PRAISE FOR *SEVEN WOMEN*

"It's the rare male who can portray women so vividly. Eric Metaxas proves he's one of the rare ones with his new book *Seven Women*."

— Kathie Lee Gifford, Emmy Award–winning host of *Today*

"Eric Metaxas offers a refreshing view of womanhood as he holds up a plumbline by which we can all measure ourselves. Faith strengthened by fire, courage to forsake personal comfort, boldness to take great risks, sacrificial compassion for others, convictions to live . . . and die . . . by, are just some of the common denominators of *Seven Women*. Although I don't measure up, this book makes me proud to take my stand as a Christian woman."

— Anne Graham Lotz, author and speaker (www.annegrahamlotz.org)

"Some authors give us words that are delicious to read. Others provide content that is good and necessary. Eric Metaxas consistently brings us the rare gift of both at the same time. If we are pulled toward complacency or discouragement, Eric gives an irresistible push toward hope and inspiration. 'If they could do it then, we can do it now! Here am I, send me!' We need to be inspired—*breathed into*. We need the wind of God in our sails for our time. In *Seven Women*, the familiar breeze is stirring again."

— Twila Paris, singer-songwriter and author

"In writing about these seven singular, extraordinary women, Eric Metaxas does honor to all women. I finished *Seven Women* feeling more blessed and encouraged in simply being a woman than ever before. The accomplishments of these women—from across time and circumstances—have indelibly shaped the world we know today. Their stories will educate, encourage, and inspire every reader. This might be the best book you read this year."

— Karen Swallow Prior, author of *Booked: Literature in the Soul of Me* and *Fierce Convictions—The Extraordinary Life of Hannah More: Poet, Reformer, Abolitionist*

"What we have in *Seven Women* is a great biographer, Eric Metaxas, writing, with his inimitable genius for depicting moral greatness, about the lives of seven great women. Once you have read *Seven Women*, you will: a) understand what makes male and female greatness both similar and—even more importantly in an age that depicts men and women as essentially identical—different; b) wonder why you didn't know about all of these women before; and c) implore Eric Metaxas to immediately write a biography of seven more women. That's how good *Seven Women* is."

— Dennis Prager, nationally syndicated
radio talk show host and columnist,
New York Times bestselling author

"To say that Eric Metaxas is an inspiration would be an understatement. It's not very often I come across a book such as *Seven Women* that has such a profound impact on my life. Eric's ability to engage readers through the lives of these seven women will not only empower you, but will ignite a fire in you to know that we as human beings all have the power to impact the world."

— April Hernandez Castillo, film and
television actress and speaker

"Religion poisons everything—except, it seems, for the untold people touched by the lives of these seven incredible women. Your jaw will drop as you read these portraits of courage, each inspired by a personal vision of God and a convictional embrace of self-sacrifice. Metaxas's beautifully written book answers the question: How can you change the world? The answer: find seven women, turn them loose, and watch Satan tremble in their presence."

— Owen Strachan, author, *The Colson
Way*

"Eric Metaxas's *Seven Women* is the encouragement and inspiration to rally on as a woman trying to make a difference in our culture. The women Eric chose gave me more energy than any protein shake. This book will be required reading for my four daughters."

— Carolyn Copeland, Broadway
producer, *Amazing Grace: The
Musical*

"Eric Metaxas writes *Seven Women* with a tender brotherly love—both in his admiration and gratitude for the women he profiles and with his challenge to men not to overlook this book and a culture to reconsider its view of women's greatness. As he's been known to do, Metaxas reintroduces some lost fundamentals here and urges us to be better by showing how it's done."

— Kathryn Jean Lopez, senior fellow,
National Review Institute

"I was one of those who hoped Eric would write *Seven Women*, not only because I loved *Seven Men* but because I knew it would be a book I would want my daughters to read. It is. Eric celebrates these women not only as remarkable people who happened to be women, but as remarkable because they were women. I can't wait to read this with my girls."

— John Stonestreet, speaker and
fellow, Colson Center for Christian
Worldview

"What a felicitous idea to write a book about women who lived up to their noble and great mission in marriage, the family, and the world. Eric Metaxas is responding to an urgent call: to reawaken women who have fallen into the trap of feminism—a murderer of chivalry—to wake up and thank God for being privileged to have the same sex as the mother of Christ."

— Dame Alice von Hildebrand, Catholic
philosopher, theologian, and
professor emerita at Hunter College

"Here is a biographer who is refreshingly and unashamedly attentive to the moral and spiritual qualities of great leaders. In these deftly written accounts, Eric Metaxas reminds us why each of these unforgettable women delivered such a bracing challenge to the spirit of their age, why each represents a unique profile in courage. A careful study of their lives and careers would be a tonic to the leadership crisis that besets our own day."

— Joseph Loconte, professor at the King's
College and author of *A Hobbit, a
Wardrobe, and a Great War*

"Metaxas makes these women come alive. I can't help wanting to gather them all in a room and ask a million questions. . . . Until that group meeting happens, this book is the next best thing."

— Joy Eggerichs, director of Love and
Respect Now

"Eric Metaxas's new book *Seven Women* demonstrates, once again, Eric's incredible gift for storytelling. In the span of only a paragraph or two, he skillfully draws the reader into a narrative that is at once informative, historical, observational, and even whimsical."

— Marybeth Hicks, author, columnist, and speaker

"Metaxas has done it again, bringing renewed insight into these women from across the centuries! Men as well as women will benefit from reading about the struggles that made these women great, the crucibles that shaped their character, and the greatness that comes from simple, deep faith."

— Chuck Roberts, pastor, Peachtree Presbyterian Church

SEVEN WOMEN

SEVEN WOMEN

AND THE SECRET OF
THEIR GREATNESS

ERIC METAXAS

NELSON
BOOKS

An Imprint of Thomas Nelson

Published in Nashville, Tennessee, by Nelson Books, an imprint of Thomas Nelson. Nelson Books and Thomas Nelson are registered trademarks of HarperCollins Christian Publishing, Inc.

Thomas Nelson titles may be purchased in bulk for educational, business, fund-raising, or sales promotional use. For information, please email SpecialMarkets@ThomasNelson.com.

Scripture quotations are from the New King James Version. Copyright © 1982 by Thomas Nelson. Used by permission. All rights reserved.

Chapter opening photo credits: Maria Skobtsova: Art Resource Photo; Hannah More: Art Resource Photo; Corrie ten Boom: Corrie ten Boom House Foundation; Susanna Wesley: Granger Images; Mother Teresa: Art Resource Photo; Joan of Arc: Bridgeman Images; Rosa Parks: Public Domain

Library of Congress Control Number: 2015942142

ISBN: 978-0-7180-2183-2 (HC)

ISBN: 978-0-7180-3729-1 (IE)

Printed in the United States of America

15 16 17 18 19 RRD 6 5 4 3 2 1

FOR SUSANNE

Contents

Introduction

Before I wrote this book, I wrote two long biographies, one about Dietrich Bonhoeffer[1] and one about William Wilberforce.[2] I was overwhelmed at the response to these books. It was clear that these stories had deeply impacted and inspired many readers, and though I knew the stories of many other extraordinary and inspiring figures, I didn't plan to write any more long biographies. But then I realized that I could write shorter ones—and so I wrote *Seven Men*.[3] The response to this book was also beyond what I had expected or hoped and further confirmed my belief that there is a great hunger for heroes in our culture.

Although I was never sure whether I would write a book that included the biographies of seven women, people kept asking me about it, and the more I thought about it, the more I knew that I must do it. I've always admired the women in this book and realized that many people didn't know their stories. To be clear, in neither *Seven Men* nor this book is the list of seven persons in any way definitive. There are many other inspiring men and women I might have included. For each book I simply chose seven people whose stories I found most compelling and inspiring—and there's no doubt that the stories of the seven great women in this book are hugely inspiring, and not just to women. I hope men will read these stories and not deny themselves the inspiration of these truly extraordinary lives. For the many men whose view of women has been twisted and dented by our cultural assumptions, these lives will be inspiring and encouraging news.

But whose stories should I tell? I began asking friends for suggestions and soliciting their thoughts. In doing so I encountered an assumption about women's greatness that wasn't surprising, but that is worth mentioning here. Many people suggested women who were the first ones to do something that men had already done. Amelia Earhart, who was the first woman to fly solo across the Atlantic in 1932, was mentioned, as was Sally Ride, who was the first American woman in space. No one mentioned Shirley "Cha Cha" Muldowney, who was the first female Top Fuel dragster champion, but I'm sure she would have come up eventually. But what these women had accomplished didn't exemplify the kind of greatness I had in mind— neither for men nor women. If it had, in writing *Seven Men* I would have replaced Wilberforce and Bonhoeffer with John Glenn and Charles Lindbergh—and might have replaced Pope John Paul II with Don "Big Daddy" Garlits or perhaps even Don "The Snake" Prudhomme, two of the greatest drag racers in history.

What struck me as wrong about these suggestions was that they presumed women should somehow be compared to men. But it seemed wrong to view great women in that way. The great men in *Seven Men* were not measured against women, so why should the women in *Seven Women* be measured against men? I wondered what was behind this way of seeing things, that women should be defined against men? Or that men and women should even be compared to each other?

Two interrelated attitudes seemed at play. First, men and women are in some ways interchangeable, that what one does the other should do. Second, women are in some kind of competition with men, and for women to progress they need to compete with men. This thinking pretends to put men and women on equal footing, but it actually only pits them against each other in a kind of zero-sum competition in which they usually tear each other down.

When I consider the seven women I chose, I see that most of them were great for reasons that derive precisely from their being women, not in spite of it; and what made them great has nothing to do with their being measured against or competing with men. In other words, their accomplishments are not gender-neutral but are rooted in their singularity as women. All of them existed and thrived as women and stand quite apart from anything touching the kind of thinking I encountered.

The first woman I chose, Joan of Arc, is a good example. She is sometimes thought of as great because she did what men do—she donned armor and became a warrior—but that is far off the mark. Joan of Arc was no fierce amazon. Far from it. There was nothing even slightly "manly" about her. On the contrary, it was her youth, innocence, purity, and holiness that made it possible for her to do what she did. Only just past girlhood she was deeply affected by the suffering she saw in the battles around her, never becoming inured to the carnage and agonies of war, as a male soldier typically will do. It was precisely her vulnerability and womanly virtue that stunned and inspired the rough soldiers in a way that no man ever could do. It was because of these qualities that they were in awe of her and respected her. Though her spirit was as large as anyone's who has ever lived, she herself was neither big nor strong. In other words, there could never be a male Joan of Arc. The very idea is a laughable oxymoron.

Similarly, Rosa Parks was specifically chosen to do what she did because she was a woman. Those who wanted to make a federal case out of her arrest knew they must have the right person, and they knew it must be a woman. Her feminine dignity was vital to the case, so there never could have been a male Rosa Parks. Obviously Susanna Wesley—who bore nineteen children and raised the surviving ten—could not have been a man; and Saint Maria of Paris wanted to be a mother to all she encountered and positively exuded motherhood.

Hannah More was considered a model of femininity by those who knew her, and because of this she was especially valued and respected by the many men whom she called friends. She was nothing like their male friends, and so the cultural influence she wielded was not a result of her being "one of the boys." Quite the contrary. Corrie ten Boom exudes an unmistakably feminine warmth; and who can doubt that it was Mother Teresa's femaleness that flummoxed and disarmed and charmed those with whom she dealt? Can we as easily imagine a man doing what she did?

So the stories of these great women show us that men and women are not interchangeable. There are things men can and should do that women cannot, and there are things that women can and should do that men cannot. So comparing men and women is something like comparing apples and oranges, except apples and oranges are actually far more like each other than are men and women. Apples and oranges can exist without each other, but men and women cannot. Men and women were deliberately designed to be different. Indeed we are specifically created as complements to each other, as different halves of a whole, and that whole reflects the glory of God. It's patently obvious that we were physically created to fit together, and of course if that weren't the case, we could not create life. So when men cease to be such or when women deny their uniqueness, they make that complementarity impossible, and the whole, as it were, suffers. There's much to be said on that subject, but the point to make here is that we are meant to be different and God wants us to celebrate and rejoice in our differences, never to suppress them or denigrate them.

'm privileged to be friends with someone whose husband was born in 1889. For context, that's the year Vincent van Gogh painted *Starry Night*, Jefferson Davis died, and Adolph Hitler was born. Alice von Hildebrand—her friends call her Lily—is a delight, so much so that I've now twice had her as my guest at Socrates in the City,[4] a forum that encourages busy and successful professionals in thinking about the bigger questions in life. Her age (ninety-one as I write this) gives her a great measure of authority, but it hasn't dimmed her fire even slightly. It would not be inaccurate to describe her as a pistol. I mention her now because she has written two books that deal with the issue of men and women. One is *The Privilege of Being a Woman*,[5] and the other is *Man and Woman: A Divine Invention*.[6] As she fiercely declared in my most recent interview with her,[7] she is tremendously pro-woman—and she was that evening we spoke—but she also makes it abundantly clear that it is precisely for this reason that she is a devoted and lifelong opponent of feminism. She firmly believes feminism to be anti-woman because it pressures women to become more like men. Everyone who heard her speak that evening was surprised, but we were sternly schooled by Dame von Hildebrand on this subject.

The lesson in all this is that to pit women against men is a form of denigration of women, as though their measure must be determined by masculine standards. The worst standards of masculine value—power usually at the top of those long lists—become the very things that some women are told they must aspire to meet. How ironic that modern culture, by so often intimating power as the highest good, should force women to accept what amounts to nothing less than patriarchal thinking, in the most pejorative sense of that adjective.

Of course this is entirely understandable. Some men have misused their power and strength to harm women. As I say in the introduction to *Seven Men*, whatever God gives us is meant for us to use to bless others, and God gives men strength and power, generally speaking, only so they will use it to bless those who do not have it. But when men fail to do so, women who are victims of the worst expressions of manhood—in fact, abrogations of real manhood—feel that the only way to deal with this is to wrest that power from men. So the idea of "female empowerment" arose, until it became another ubiquitous and thought-free cliché. But the problem with this idea is that it presupposes the tremendously harmful and distorting idea of a competition for power.

That idea was famously popularized in 1973 in the so-called "Battle of the Sexes," the much-heralded and nationally televised tennis match between Billy Jean King, a woman, and Bobby Riggs, a man. The cultural climate at the time was that there were two ways of seeing the world. One was the bigoted "Male Chauvinist Pig" way, and the other was the enlightened "I Am Woman (Hear Me Roar)" way. In this scenario women and men were pitted against each other as bitter adversaries, and the only way for women to lift themselves up was to denounce men as sexists and cavemen.

Billie Jean King was then in her prime, twenty-six years younger than Bobby Riggs, who had been a tennis champion in the 1940s. That she prevailed was no great surprise to anyone paying attention, but the way the match was publicized made it out to be an epochal event. The most important and terrible thing was that it portrayed the relationship between men and women as a zero-sum game. If one won, the other lost. In this view of the relationship between the sexes, there can be no equity, no mutual admiration, no mutual encouragement, and of course, no real love. That night it was this view writ large: the only way for one to win was for the other to lose. It made for great television ratings, but this idea is a pernicious lie, one that has hurt men and women terribly.

Whether we like it or not, men and women are inextricably intertwined. Because the Bible says that we are made in God's image—"male and female He created them" (Gen. 1:27)—the fortunes of one are so linked to the fortunes of the other that there is no way to lift one without lifting the other and no way to degrade one without degrading the other. So whenever men have used their positions of authority or their power to denigrate women, they have denigrated themselves and have denied themselves the fullness of manhood God intended for them. When women have tried to ape the behavior of power-hungry men, they have degraded themselves and denied themselves the dignity of being above that vulgar fray.

It is all the more noteworthy that the great women in this volume stood on their own as women, but not in a defiant stance that pitted them against men. On the contrary, they were large-hearted enough and secure enough in who they were to show remarkable magnanimity toward men, with whom they had notably warm relationships. Joan of Arc's relationships with the soldiers who served under her is nothing less than moving; Susanna Wesley's love for her sons and their reverence for her speak volumes; Hannah More's relationships with her four sisters were at the very heart of her life, but she also had a pronounced capacity for friendship with men, including David Garrick, Horace Walpole, Dr. Samuel Johnson, and William Wilberforce. Maria Skobtsova's (Saint Maria of Paris) love for her son and relationship with Father Dimitri Klepinin tell us everything about her, as does Corrie ten Boom's relationship with her father. Mother Teresa's friendship with Pope John Paul II was well known, and it is clear that Rosa Parks's relationship with her husband was at the center of her life and accomplishments.

◆ ◆ ◆

Perhaps the best thing about biographies is that they enable us to slip the strictures of time and provide a bracing corrective to our tendency to see everything in the dark glass of our own era, with all its blind spots, motes, beams, and distortions. We must be honest enough to recognize that each era cannot help having a pinched, parochial view of things, and of course the largest part of that parochialism is that each era thinks it is not parochial at all. Each era has the fatal hubris to believe that it has once and for all climbed to the top of the mountain and can see everything as it is, from the highest and most objective vantage point possible. But to assert that ours is the only blinker-less view of things is to blither fatuousness. We need to delve into the past to know that we have not progressed to any point of perfection and objectivity, and in examining the lives of these seven women, we are doing just that. We see that our view of many things, not least our view of how women can be great, is fatally tinged by our own cultural assumptions. The Bible says we are to humble ourselves, and in reading the stories of great men and women from the past, we inevitably do just that. But in humbling ourselves in that way we ironically gain a far greater objectivity and a far better vantage point from which to see things.

May the true stories of these seven great women help you to see yourself and your own time and world all the more clearly.

— Eric Metaxas
New York City
July 2014

ONE

Joan of Arc

1412–1431

E ven to those who know it well, the story of the woman called Joan of Arc is an enigma. I knew little about her until I saw the landmark silent film *The Passion of Joan of Arc*[1] some years ago. But after seeing the film and reading more about her, I quickly understood that her character and her exploits were so extraordinary as to be almost beyond belief. They are certainly without equal. But what are we to make of this woman? Those who would make her out to be an early feminist, or a religious fanatic, or a lunatic subject to strange delusions may be forgiven their confusion, because—although she was none of those things—her life stands well apart from all others. She was so pure and so brave and so singular in her faith and obedience to God that, perhaps like Francis of Assisi or even like Jesus himself, she challenges many of our deepest assumptions about what a life can be.

To get a sense of who Joan of Arc was, imagine a teenage farm girl entering the halls of the Pentagon in Washington, DC, and forcefully

1

demanding to see the secretary of defense, saying that God had given her a plan to end all terrorism aimed at the United States and her allies, and all she required was an army of soldiers with weapons. Most people would sensibly assume such a young woman was mentally ill or perhaps simply extremely naive. The last thing we would imagine is that she was actually sent by God, and that everything she said was true and would come to pass precisely as she said it would. But this was approximately the scenario that faced French military and political figures in 1429, when a humble, uneducated seventeen-year-old girl from a small village appeared before them.

In order to appreciate what this girl was proposing, we have to understand the situation in France at that time. The war that came to be known as the Hundred Years War had been raging on and off since 1337. The English, having taken over vast tracts of France by 1429, were winning, and they now hoped to literally crown their efforts by putting an English king on the French throne. At the time, this practically seemed a *fait accompli*. But Joan innocently and forcefully explained to French officials that she had been sent by God to drive the English out of the great city of Orléans. What's more, she claimed that she would ensure that the proper Frenchman—Charles VII—was crowned king of France! Taking her seriously was out of the question; and yet somehow, in the end, the befuddled and desperate leaders of France did just that. They had run out of sensible options and knew they had nothing to lose. But far less bizarre than their taking her seriously is the fact that she would actually succeed in everything she said she would do. It is preposterous to consider, and yet history records that it happened.

◆ ◆ ◆

Jeanne d'Arc—or Joan of Arc, as she is called in English—was called Jeanette by her parents. She was born in 1412 into a peasant family in Domrémy, a village in northeastern France. With her parents and four siblings, she lived in a simple stone house next to the village church.

Like most peasant girls of that time, when she was old enough Joan helped her father, Jacques, in the fields. She also took care of the family's animals, weeded the vegetable garden, and helped her mother in the house. She is said to have especially enjoyed weaving and spinning. Joan was never taught to read or write, but she had a passionate interest in the church and in God. At an early age, she prayed frequently and fervently. Long after her death her childhood companions remembered how they had teased their friend for her piety.

Life was precarious for the citizens of France. The Hundred Years War had been the agonizing backdrop of their lives for as long as anyone could remember. The English firmly believed that France should be part of England, and because of much intermarrying between the royal families of England and France, the line of succession was unclear.

The confusion started around 1392, when the French began hearing rumors that the man they considered the rightful king of France, Charles VI, was suffering bouts of madness. His uncle, Philip the Good (so-called), seized the reins of the kingdom. He and Charles's unpleasant wife, Queen Isabeau, were attempting to end the war in a way that was handsomely profitable to themselves and to England, but decidedly detrimental to France.

Philip was also the powerful Duke of Burgundy, whose lands—constituting a considerable portion of France—were under English control. He wanted France to give in to English demands in order to stop the endless fighting. Queen Isabeau went along with this plan and wheedled her mentally compromised husband into signing the Treaty of Troyes. This treaty gave Charles VI the right to rule France during his lifetime, but upon his death, Henry V of England would rule both countries. To make the provisions of the treaty more palatable, Henry V married Princess Catherine, the daughter of Charles VI and Queen Isabeau, so any children they had would be half-French.

It all might have worked, but for one person: Princess Catherine's

3

younger brother, the crown prince Charles—or the Dauphin, as the French called him—who was intent on remaining in the line of succession. In 1422, to complicate things further, King Charles VI died. But the Duke of Burgundy and Queen Isabeau's plans to have England's Henry V succeed him were no longer possible because Henry himself had died two months earlier. Who then would become the next king of France? That was the question that burned in the hearts of every Frenchman—and that burned in the heart of the inhabitants of Joan's village, Domrémy.

There were two principal contenders: the Dauphin (Charles VII) and Henry VI, the infant son of Henry V and Catherine. The English and their allies, the Burgundians, who controlled northern France, predictably supported Henry VI, while those in southern France supported the Dauphin. So the war raged on, and now the French were fighting not only the English but each other as well.

Most of the Hundred Years War had been fought on French soil, and the French had not won any significant victories in decades. By 1429, when Joan was seventeen, the English had managed to conquer a good deal of France's northern territory, and sections of southwestern France were under the control of the Anglo-allied Burgundians. The French populace had suffered greatly during the bubonic plague pandemic (the Black Death) that first spread from China to Europe in the 1340s. French merchants were cut off from foreign markets, and the French economy was in shambles.

Joan and her fellow Domrémy villagers strongly supported the Dauphin and considered the English a foul enemy, in part because it was not unusual for English soldiers to march into French villages, killing civilians, burning homes, and stealing crops and cattle. But what could they do to ensure that the Dauphin would become king? It was not something that anyone would have thought probable. But around the time Joan was twelve, something began happening that would catapult her into the center of these events and make her the principal player in leading France to victory and making the Dauphin her rightful king: she began hearing voices and seeing visions. Joan said that messengers from heaven were visiting her in her father's garden. She believed them to be the archangel Michael, Saint Catherine, and Saint Margaret. At first they didn't say anything about France or her role in saving France from the English; they just encouraged Joan in her already deep faith.

Joan looked forward to and loved her interactions with these heavenly visitors, but over time their words to her became quite specific and serious. They informed her that she had a great mission to perform. She was to rescue France from the English and take the Dauphin to the city of Reims to be crowned. Like Mary, the mother of Jesus, Joan was amazed at what these heavenly visitors told her. Who was she to lead an army? She hardly knew how to mount a horse, much less how to lead soldiers into battle. But as she was a girl of deep faith, she did not doubt that these messengers were indeed from heaven and must be taken seriously.

Joan was not the only person in the family to be troubled by things difficult to understand. One night her father dreamed that his pretty, adolescent daughter would run away with soldiers. Misunderstanding its meaning, he dramatically instructed his sons to drown their sister if she ever did such a thing. He also preemptively began to plan for Joan's marriage to a local swain. Unbeknownst to her father, however, Joan had made a private vow to God never to marry. So when the time came, she refused to go through with the ceremony, despite the fact that her so-called fiancé went to court over the broken arrangement.

When Joan was about sixteen, her "voices," as she called them, told her that her time had come at last. They gave her specific instructions to travel to the town of Vaucouleurs. Once there, she was to ask Governor Robert de Baudricourt to provide her with an armed escort to the castle of Chinon, where the Dauphin and his court lived. Knowing how her parents would react, Joan told them she wished to visit her married cousin, Jeanne Laxart, who lived a short distance from Vaucouleurs. They allowed their daughter to go.

She did visit her cousin but then talked her cousin's husband, Durand, into taking her to see Baudricourt. The governor patiently listened to Joan describe how God had instructed her to lead an army in driving the English out of France and then to oversee the crowning of the Dauphin as king of France. But what was the esteemed and dignified governor to make of this simple girl's outrageous story? He did what anyone else likely would have done: he told Durand to send her home immediately but not before boxing her ears for all the trouble she was causing.

The frustrated Joan returned home, but no sooner had she arrived than the horrors of the war finally came to her own doorstep. Burgundian soldiers swept into Domrémy and cruelly laid waste to the entire village by fire. She and her fellow villagers fled to a nearby fortified town. Then, a few months later came worse news: the English had surrounded the great French city of Orléans and were laying siege to it. Joan's voices gave her an urgent new message: God intended for her to rescue Orléans.

Joan, now seventeen, returned to Vaucouleurs and spent the next six weeks attempting to see the governor again. While waiting, she spoke openly to all who would listen about her God-given mission. The Vaucouleurs townspeople remembered a famous prophecy that France would one day be lost by a woman and then restored by a maiden—a virgin. They came to assume that the woman who would lose France was the despicable Queen Isabeau and that the maiden who would restore their country might well be Joan. As for the governor, he was less encouraging and again dismissed her and her preposterous ideas.

But Joan did not take his rebuffs to heart. "I must be at the King's side," she insisted. "There will be no help if not from me. Although I would rather have remained spinning at my mother's side . . . yet must I go and must I do this thing, for my Lord wills that I do so."[2]

There's little doubt that Joan really did wish to remain at home with her family, doing the things she had grown up doing. But she knew that God himself was calling her to the task at hand. She would not disobey, and she would not relent until she had done what God called her to do.

Baudricourt agreed to see the persistent farm girl again, but this time, Joan told him something remarkable, something she had no way of knowing. In Mark Twain's fictional account of Joan's life, which he researched and wrote for twenty years, the outspoken religious skeptic presented this account of Joan's meeting with Baudricourt:

> "In God's name, Robert de Baudricourt, you are too slow about sending me, and have caused damage thereby, for this day the Dauphin's cause has lost a battle near Orléans, and will suffer yet greater injury if you do not send me to him soon."
>
> The governor was perplexed by this speech, and said:
>
> "To-day, child, to-day? How can you know what has happened in that region to-day? It would take eight or ten days for the word to come."
>
> "My voices have brought the word to me, and it is true. A battle was lost to-day, and you are in fault to delay me so."
>
> The governor walked the floor a while, talking within himself, but letting a great oath fall outside now and then; and finally he said:
>
> "Harkye! go in peace, and wait. If it shall turn out as you say, I will give you the letter and send you to the King, and not otherwise."
>
> Joan said with fervor: "Now God be thanked, these waiting days are almost done."[3]

Word arrived that the French had indeed lost the battle. The governor was flabbergasted and finally convinced.

Orléans, located along the Loire River, was the final obstacle to an assault on the rest of France and therefore of tremendous strategic importance. Given the unlikelihood that Orléans could long endure a lengthy siege, rescue of the city was essential if France were ever to rule itself again. But to see the Dauphin, Joan would have to travel to Chinon, where the royal court had relocated from Bourges.

Joan began working out practical details of her 350-mile journey. It was for her own safety when traveling across enemy territory that she decided to cut her hair short and dress as a man. The citizens of Vaucouleurs clearly saw the sense in this and provided her with masculine clothing—a tunic, hose, boots, and spurs. They also provided her with a horse, and Baudricourt himself gave Joan her first sword.

On a cold February night, Joan—who now simply called herself "La Pucelle," which translates to "the Maid," or "the Maiden," meaning a young woman or a virgin—swung herself atop her horse and began the long journey to Chinon, accompanied by six male escorts. They had agreed to travel by night and sleep by day in order to avoid enemy soldiers, whom they might otherwise encounter, as they rode through hostile Burgundian lands.

Eleven days later Joan and her escorts stopped in Fierbois, a three-hour ride from Chinon. There Joan dictated a letter to the Dauphin, asking to meet with him. The Dauphin agreed, and soon the little band clattered onto the cobblestoned streets of Chinon. Joan was met by many curious stares, for stories of the virgin who claimed she would save France had preceded her.

Like Robert de Baudricourt, the Dauphin had prepared a test for Joan. She had hinted in a letter that, although she had never met him, she would be able to identify the Dauphin. So Louis de Bourbon, Count of Vendôme, led Joan through a stone passage opening into the castle's grand hall, where she found herself in the company of hundreds of gorgeously dressed and bejeweled guests. After looking around for a moment, Joan walked straight toward the Dauphin and knelt before him. "God give you life, gentle king," she said.[4]

"I am not the king," the Dauphin replied. "There is the king!" he said, pointing to another man.

Joan responded, "In God's name, Sir, you *are* the King, and no other! Give me the troops wherewith to succour Orléans and to guard you to Rheims to be anointed and crowned. For it is the will of God."[5]

Still not quite convinced, the Dauphin took Joan aside to speak privately. In an effort to prove she had been sent by God, she told him about something he had done in private: he had prayed that God would reveal to him whether or not he was actually the son of Charles VI. His mother, hardly a virtuous woman, had claimed he was not. If he were not the son of the late king, the Dauphin prayed that God would take away his desire to rule.

The Dauphin was overjoyed when Joan told him that he was, indeed, of royal blood; she said that she knew this because her voices had told her. He then gave Joan a room in Chinon Castle's Tower of Coudray, along with a household staff, including a young page, who, all his long life afterward, recalled Joan's "prayers and her fervor."[6] She was also given a knight, John d'Aulon, and a chaplain, John Pasquerel, who later wrote a lively biography of her. Among the men who met with Joan was Jean d'Alençon, the celebrated Duke of Alençon and a cousin to the king, of whom Joan became fond, calling him her "handsome duke."

But not all the king's men were impressed with Joan. Georges de La Trémoille, Count of de Guînes, who had substantial influence over the Dauphin, said that he "found it absurd . . . that so young a girl of low birth, unlettered, lately come from nothingness, should play the leader."[7]

It was he and other advisers who urged the Dauphin to investigate Joan's background and claims and determine whether these voices of hers came from heaven or hell. Additional precious weeks passed as Joan was thoroughly investigated. She was required to travel to Poitiers, a university town, where the council of church scholars examined her. These men insisted she perform a miracle, which she refused to do. She might have told them about the miracle of her knowing the Dauphin's secret worries about his legitimacy, which he had confirmed, but she chose not to embarrass him by doing so.

The Dauphin's advisers remained skeptical. But Joan had no doubt about what God had told her and had grown impatient. "In the name of God," she replied, "I came not here to Poitiers to work miracles. At

Orléans you will see miracle enough. With a few men or with many, to Orléans will I go."[8]

Joan then prophesied to them that four events would take place. She said, "Orléans I shall relieve. The Dauphin I shall crown in Rheims. Paris will come back to its true king. The Duke of Orléans, captive in the Tower of London, will return home."[9]

In the end they agreed that the Dauphin would accept Joan's help. By then, as biographers Regine Pernoud and Véronique Clin put it, Joan "had come to personify hope, the type of hope that (according to the witnesses of her time) the distressed kingdom no longer maintained—that is, the hope of divine assistance."[10] She was given a military retinue consisting of a steward, pages, two heralds, messengers, and her brothers, John and Peter, along with the equipment she would need as the leader of an army. She was fitted out with a specially designed suit of armor, and the Dauphin himself gave her a magnificent horse.

Joan also required a standard. This flag was necessary so that soldiers would have a way of recognizing their commander when his—or her—visor was down, as it must be during the fighting. Joan explained that the voices had described to her just how it should appear. It should be made of "fine white linen, with the lilies of the realm scattered on it and sewn, and there was to be painted on it the figure of Our Lord with the world in His hand, and on either side two angels adoring, with the motto: 'Jesus, Mary.'" On Joan's blue shield was painted a white dove holding in its beak a scroll, upon which were written the words "By command of the King of Heaven."[11]

Joan already had a sword. Nonetheless she sent a letter to the priests of the shrine of Saint Catherine de Fierbois, the place where she had prayed while waiting to travel to Chinon. She told them to dig behind the altar, where they would discover a rusted sword that was engraved with five crosses. Her voices had told her the sword was there, and *mirabile dictu*—indeed it was. The priests dug and found it, removed the rust, and then sent it to Joan. The Maid did not intend to ever harm anyone with the sword. It was, she said, intended merely to be a symbol of command.

Joan began giving commands to her soldiers, instructions that probably astonished these rough men. She made it clear that the army she commanded would be God's army in every way. She told the men that they must not swear and must confess their sins. They also were to be just in everything they did. And although they would indeed be conquerors, they must not do what soldiers in those days almost always did: loot the villagers' homes and burn them. Joan personally chased "immoral women" from the camp. Her army also included priests, who morning and evening were assembled to sing hymns to the Virgin Mary.

Having a female leader, and a young one at that, was a new and challenging experience for the French soldiers. An eyewitness to the attitudes of the soldiers who fought under Joan's command, Gobert Thibault, described the phenomenon of an innocent young girl living among virile men: "I heard many of those closest to her say that they had never had any desire for her; that is to say, they sometimes felt a certain carnal urge but never dared to let themselves go with her, and they believed that it was not possible to desire her; I have questioned several of those who sometimes slept the night in Joan's company about this, and they answered as I have, adding that they had never felt any carnal desire when they saw her."[12]

Before engaging in the Battle of Orléans, Joan sent a letter to English leaders during Holy Week of 1429, urging them to "surrender to the Maid, who is sent here from God, the King of Heaven, the keys to all of the good cities that you have taken and violated in France.... She is entirely ready to make peace," it read, "if you are willing to settle accounts with her, provided that you give up France and pay for having occupied her."[13]

In the letter she ordered English troops to leave France and warned, "If you do not do so, I am commander of the armies, and in whatever place I shall meet your French allies, I shall make them leave it, whether they wish to or not; and if they will not obey, I shall have them all killed. . . . If you do not wish to believe this message from God through the Maid, then wherever we find you we will strike you there, and make a great uproar greater than any made in France for a thousand years."[14]

The English were not impressed. They warned Joan that if they caught her, they would burn her at the stake. Joan and her troops likely assembled at the Blois fortress on the Loire, about halfway between Tours and Orléans. Both Tours and Blois were controlled by the French. The English controlled the Loire's right bank, upriver. Joan's confessor, John Pasquerel, described this moment: "They marched out on the side of the Solonge [the south bank of the Loire] . . . camped in the fields that night and the following day as well. On the third day, they arrived near Orléans, where the English had set up their siege along the bank of the Loire. And the king's soldiers came so close to the English that Englishmen and Frenchmen could see one another within easy reach."[15]

Joan was about to meet the man who would become her great ally: Jean d'Orléans, the Count of Dunois, known throughout his life as the Bastard of Orléans because he was the illegitimate half brother of the Duke of Orléans. But this Bastard, alas, believing he knew far more about battle tactics than a teenage girl, had deceived Joan. He was now in charge of Orléans troops (because his half brother, the duke, was being held prisoner in London). He arranged for Joan's soldiers to make a long detour, causing them to come in "well arrayed up to the banks of the Loire on the Sologne side."[16] He had decided on this detour in order to keep clear of the English, who had staked out positions in the vicinity of Orléans. But Joan, eager to begin fighting, discovered that she and her men had been duped and had in fact bypassed Orléans.

Joan was livid and gave the Bastard a tongue-lashing he would never forget. Approaching him on horseback, she asked, "Are you the one who gave orders for me to come here, on this side of the river, so that I could not go directly to [General John] Talbot and the English?"

As the Bastard recalled later, "I answered that I, and others, including the wisest men around me, had given this advice, believing it best and safest."

"In God's name," Joan replied, "the counsel of Our Lord God is wiser and safer than yours. You thought that you could fool me, and instead you fooled yourself; I bring you better help than ever came to you from any soldier to any city: It is the help of the King of Heaven."[17]

The English soldiers had camped mainly along the Loire outside the western gate of Orléans. Joan said the English would not come out from their forts or their camp, and she was right. Their strength was insufficient, so for the time being they stayed with their guns, waiting for reinforcements to arrive. If she had gone there when she had wanted to, her forces would have had the advantage.

Joan at last made a triumphal entry into the besieged city on the evening of April 29, 1429, accompanied by the Bastard and many other noblemen and men at arms. The crowds, holding torches high, cheered and reached up to touch her as she made her way from the Burgundy Gate across the city to the home of Jacques Boucher, today the Maison de Jeanne d'Arc. Seeing the famous Maid gave the people tremendous hope. She was wise beyond her years and yet innocent; she was strong and vulnerable; she was bold and humble. She was all these things at once, and she seemed to embody France itself, and hope itself too.

Joan lodged at Boucher's home and spent the next nine days impatiently waiting to go into battle. The Bastard had convinced her to wait until reinforcements arrived from the Dauphin. She twice went out to stand on the bridge of Orléans and trade insults with the English; she urged them to surrender or be slaughtered. The English in turn called her a cow-herd and insulted her soldiers with crude epithets.

In the meantime, the Bastard had ridden out to meet the French reinforcements, and when he returned he had news: a new English army, commanded by the famous captain John Fastolf, had been sent to Orléans to lead the battle against them. Joan was delighted that at last the battle would begin, but she took no chances that the Bastard might again deceive her. Turning to him, she warned, "Bastard, O

Bastard, in God's name, I order you, as soon as you know of Fastolf's coming, to let me know it!"[18] He promised that he would.

But when the first short skirmish occurred, Joan was asleep, and nobody thought to wake her. The Bastard took the army to attack the fortress at Saint-Loup. Joan suddenly awoke, telling her steward, Jean d'Aulon, that her voices had told her to "go against the English,"[19] but she was unsure whether this meant she should attack their fortifications or Fastolf, who was coming to resupply them.

After lashing out at her page for neglecting to wake her while French blood was being spilled, Joan shouted for her horse to be readied and her standard brought while she dressed quickly. She then rode to the Burgundy Gate, where a battle was raging. As soon as the French forces saw Joan, their spirits soared. They raised a shout and managed to take both the *bastide* (fortified town) and the fortress itself. In terms of territory, the victory was rather insignificant, but the revitalizing effect it had on French forces was extraordinary.

The brutal reality of war, however, which Joan had never before seen, greatly disturbed her, and when she saw the many wounded and dead French soldiers, she wept. Joan went to confession afterward and urged her fellow soldiers to "confess their sins publicly and to give thanks to God for the victory that He had granted."[20]

Two days later Joan was readying herself for combat when she ran into Raoul de Gaucourt, the governor of Orléans, who told her he would not allow her to make an attack that day because the captains did not want her to do so. But Joan was defiant. "[W]hether you wish it or not," she told him, "the men-at-arms will come and gain what they gained the other day."[21]

So Joan and her soldiers crossed the Loire. The Maid led her troops to the left bank, where the English had erected another bastide. But then she saw that it was deserted. The English had escaped up river to a second bastide, one that was stronger. The English withdrawal made a French advance more dangerous, but Joan rode toward them nonetheless. An eyewitness, Jean d'Aulon, noted:

When they perceived that the enemy was coming out of the Bastide of the Augustinians to rush upon them, the Maid and La Hire, who were always in front of their men to protect them, immediately couched their lances and led the attack upon the enemy. Everyone followed them, and they began to strike the enemy in such a manner that they constrained them by sheer force to withdraw and to return to the Bastide. . . . With great diligence, they assailed that bastide from all directions so that they seized it and took it by assault quickly. The greater part of the enemy were killed or captured.[22]

Joan had again won a tremendous victory, but once more the Dauphin and his counselors dithered about what to do next. They complained that there were too few French and too many English. The city of Les Tourelles was well provisioned with food, they said, so why not simply guard it while waiting for the king's help?

Joan would have none of it. She ordered Pasquerel to rise early the next day, May 7, 1430, and prepare for battle. They would attack the fortress of Les Tourelles. She prophesied that she would be wounded in the fighting above the left breast, but that the wound would not be fatal, and the French would take Les Tourelles. This was precisely what happened.

The great Anglo-French writer and historian Hilaire Belloc described the battle: "The stone walls of the rampart swarmed with the scaling ladders full of men hurled down [under an assault of arrows] and assault upon assault repelled, and the Maid in the midst with her banner; when, at noon, a shaft struck right through the white shoulder plate over her left breast and she fell."[23] .

Joan bravely pulled the arrow out herself, had the wound treated with olive oil, rested awhile, and then leapt back into the fray. By nightfall the soldiers had spent thirteen exhausting hours in battle. The English were certain of victory, especially when they heard the Bastard's trumpets sounding retreat. But Joan had no doubt that the French would win. After going away for a time of prayer while her exhausted men rested and had something to eat, Joan convinced the Bastard to make one final assault. Holding her standard high so that her men could see it in the fading light, she shouted, "When the flag touches the stone, all is yours!"[24] The weary soldiers rose to the occasion magnificently, breaking down the English defenses and pouring over the walls.

The English ran for their lives toward a wooden drawbridge, but the French had torched a boat and sent it floating beneath the bridge. It caught fire. As the English raced across it, a portion collapsed. All those soldiers who fell into the water in their heavy armor drowned. The citizens of Orléans came forward to patch the bridge with ladders and planks then rushed across the structure "to attack the fort from the rear, setting it on fire with flaming arrows."[25] At last the towers fell, and everyone within the fortress was killed or taken prisoner.

It was a tremendous victory, so great that today, nearly six hundred years later, the French still celebrate it every May 7. Despite her injury Joan visited the bridge that night to see the rejoicing of the citizens of newly freed Orléans. From his position on the far side of the river, the English general, Lord Talbot, heard bells of celebration ringing through the night. He pulled his troops out of the remaining forts that surrounded Orléans.

Orléans was relieved, just as Joan had prophesied. Now she must crown France's rightful king at Reims. The following day she and the Bastard rode to the castle of Loches to meet the Dauphin, who was overjoyed to see her. She urged him to travel immediately to Reims, the traditional place for crowning French kings. But again the Dauphin's counselors were unwilling to act quickly. They would spend nearly two weeks debating what should be done next. She continued to press the Dauphin to act. Her voices had told her that she would have only a year to achieve her goals. "Dauphin, noble Dauphin," she said, "linger not here in council with many words, but come to Reims and be crowned! For the voice calls to me: 'Go forward, Daughter of God; I am with you. Go! Go!'"[26]

In the end the Dauphin was finally convinced, and the army set out to clear the towns for his unimpeded passage to Reims. The objective of the Loire campaign, commanded by the Duke of Alençon, "was to dislodge the enemy from their entrenched positions on the banks of the Loire River and in the plains to the north, in order to protect the rear of the army when it departed for Reims."[27]

But Reims was roughly twice as far away as Paris and deep within enemy territory, so the idea that the Maid and her soldiers would travel there was unthinkable to the English. They assumed the French would do the sensible thing and attack Normandy or attempt to recapture Paris.

It was a stunning campaign, taking just one week. First, the French captured Jargeau, the town to which the English had fled following their rout at Orléans. Joan "stood to see the firing of the great gun brought from Orléans, and when . . . a tower fell, [the Duke of] Alençon dreaded the breach, thinking it not wide enough yet and too high piled with stone; but she said to him: 'To the Breach and fear nothing! This is the hour of God's pleasure; and do you not remember how I told your wife in Tours that I would bring you home?'"[28]

Joan was injured during this battle when she attempted to scale a ladder. A stone struck her helmet, causing her to tumble to the ground. But she quickly recovered and shouted to her men: "On, friends, on! Hearts high! We have them in this hour!"[29]

Once again inspired by the Maid, her soldiers captured the town. Many English lost their lives, and the English leader, the Duke of Suffolk, was captured. Then Joan and the Duke of Alençon rode triumphantly back to Orléans. By now, her reputation was such that English-held towns simply opened their gates to her. With no effort, her soldiers took the towns of Meung-sur-Loire and Beaugency.

But at last the army of Sir John Fastolf had arrived, and Lord Talbot would have help. Their combined forces marched confidently toward the French in what would be remembered as the Battle of Patay. The French victory on June 18 was a rout, one of inconceivable and absurd proportions. History records that the French lost three men, while the casualties on the English side numbered more than four thousand.

When Joan and her army returned victorious to Orléans, the citizens erupted with jubilation. She would at last travel with the Dauphin to Reims to crown him king. But again his court wrung their hands and delayed his departure. There were still some walled cities held by the Burgundians, they said, so they did not think the Dauphin should make the trip. She went to him and urged him to go to Reims immediately. He must be crowned king, she said, and soon! The Dauphin thanked her for her victories on his behalf but suggested she first rest before they make the journey. She knew this would be a mistake and persisted. Finally the Dauphin relented, and in late June, Joan and her men set out for Reims, with the Dauphin following two days later.

Upon the Dauphin's arrival in Reims on July 16, the citizens cheered themselves hoarse for joy. Even Joan's father and mother had traveled there to witness the great, almost incredible accomplishment of their daughter. Two of her brothers had come as well. But even in the midst of this long-sought climax, she was already looking forward to what lay ahead. The following morning, as preparations went forward for the coronation, she dictated a letter to the Duke of Burgundy, demanding that he make a "firm and lasting peace with the king of France."

"You two must pardon one another fully with a sincere heart, as loyal Christians should," she added. "I must make known to you from the King of Heaven, my rightful and sovereign Lord, for your good and for your honor and upon your life, that you will win no more battles against loyal Frenchmen."[30]

Later that day, to shouts of acclamation, the Dauphin rode his horse into the Cathedral of Reims itself, there to be crowned king. And standing beside the Dauphin was the humble Maid whose faith and fire had brought it all to pass. As the crown was set upon the Dauphin's head, Joan knelt beside the man who now, in this moment, was officially King Charles VII. With tears running down her face, she said, "High-born King, now is the will of God accomplished. For He it was who ordained that I should free Orléans and bring you here to this city of Reims for your sacring, to blazon it forth that you are Rightful Lord. And now the Realm of France is yours."[31]

As a reward for her services to him, King Charles granted Joan's wish that her home village of Domrémy be forever exempt from paying taxes. That was all she had asked, and this promise was kept for four centuries.

Tragically, however, this weak monarch would in a very short time betray the noble woman who had done so much to place the crown of France upon his head.

◆ ◆ ◆

The crowning of Charles would have significant consequences. Cities that had been under the control of the English-allied Burgundians were now prepared to recognize Charles as their rightful ruler. And Joan's army, under the command of the Duke of Alençon, was eager to take back Paris—just as she had prophesied—and not only that, but to drive the English out of all of France once and for all.

Joan had not once failed in her advice to the king; all she had said had, in fact, come to pass. Nonetheless, Charles and his advisers didn't trust her instincts. They had ideas of winning the war in other, easier ways. They hoped to persuade the Duke of Burgundy to break his alliance with the English and to join the French side. They did not tell Joan that the king had agreed to a fifteen-day truce with the Duke of Burgundy, wherein the duke had promised to surrender Paris at the conclusion of that time. In truth, the deceptive duke would double-cross them. He had only bought time with his lie and was awaiting the arrival of reinforcements from England—some thirty-five hundred of them.

When Joan became aware of the truce, she was immediately suspicious, so on August 5, she wrote to the citizens of Reims:

It's true that the King has made a truce with the Duke of Burgundy lasting fifteen days, by which he [Burgundy] must turn over the city of Paris peaceably at the end of fifteen days. However, do not be surprised if I don't enter it [Paris] so quickly. I am not at all content with truces made like this, and I don't know if I will uphold them; but if I do uphold them it will only be in order to protect the honor of the King; also, they [the Burgundians] will not cheat the Royal family, for I will maintain and keep the King's army together so as to be ready at the end of these fifteen days if they don't make peace.[32]

In the meantime Joan and the French army marched through towns near Paris, in each case not having to fight but accepting a peaceful surrender.

Joan knew that attacking Paris would be difficult, much more so than the Battle of Orléans. Paris was well fortified and even surrounded by a moat. But she was undeterred. As she had always done before attacking, she shouted to the English to surrender or die; and as they had before previous battles, they vowed to fight.

On September 8, the French forces under Joan's leadership began the attack. At one point, she decided that she herself would determine the depth of the moat. But just as she was dipping her lance into the moat's water, an arrow from an English crossbow struck her in the thigh, in the very place where her armor did not protect her. Lying on the ground in pain, she urged her soldiers to leave her where she was and continue the battle, but the Raoul de Gaucourt and others came to her and carried her off, ending the assault.

It is worth noting that Joan had not received any instructions from her voices regarding this battle and was now acting on her own initiative. She was never to receive their advice again regarding battle tactics.

The next day brought terrible news. King Charles himself had ordered that they cease the assault on Paris altogether. Once again the timorous, irresolute Charles had been influenced to take this stand by his advisers—particularly Grand Chamberlain Georges de la Trémoille, who disliked Joan.

The Maid's brief but remarkable military career was now nearing its end. Her voices had warned her in June that she would soon be captured, that she should "take it favorably,"[33] and that God would aid her.

In October Joan's army captured Saint-Pierre-le-Moûtier but failed to take La Charité-sur-Loire. King Charles had signed a truce with England, leaving a frustrated Joan idle—until the truce ended the following spring. In May 1430 English and Burgundian forces attacked Compiègne, and Joan traveled there with a small force of four hundred men to take part in the city's defense.

During the May 23 battle the French, seeing six thousand Burgundian reinforcements approaching and fearing that they would be overwhelmed, rushed onto the bridge of boats that Guillaume de Flavy had strung out across the Oise. Joan, who never withdrew without regret, protected their retreat. Perceval de Cagney later described what happened: "During that time, the captain of the place, seeing the great multitude of Burgundians and Englishmen ready to get on the bridge, out of fear that he would lose his position, raised the drawbridge of the city and closed the gate. So the Maid remained outside and only a few of her men were with her."[34] Joan fought the enemy bravely until one of them yanked her off her horse and threw her to the ground.

Biographers have their doubts about this description. Pernoud and Clin, for example, noted that it was not "the main gate of the city that had been closed but a gate in the curtain wall, which was not vital to the defense of the city proper and which presumably cut off the combatants' retreat. This is why—though reasonable skepticism persists—some believe that Joan's fear of betrayal was fulfilled."[35]

Joan now became a prisoner of Lionel of Wandomme, a lieutenant of John of Luxembourg, who was, in turn, under the Duke of Burgundy's control. Lionel transported her to Margny-lès-Compiègne, where she was kept under guard in a tower at Beaurevoir Castle until November.

The English, who had come to believe they would never win glory on the field of battle while the Maid lived, rejoiced at her capture and immediately began pressuring the Duke of Burgundy to hand her over to them. The duke eventually agreed, accepting a ransom of ten thousand francs, in addition to six thousand francs for the soldiers who had actually captured the Maid.

Joan far preferred death to being given over to the English, and while these negotiations regarding her fate took place, she seems to have wished to end her life, leaping from the seventy-foot-high tower in which she was being held. But somehow she survived, landing on a patch of soft earth. She was discovered unconscious hours later and returned to her cell, having escaped not only death, but injury. This was one of several efforts she made to escape. But now one of her voices—she said it was Saint Catherine—told Joan to "confess myself and ask pardon from God for having jumped."[36]

King Charles had initially promised vengeance for the capture of Joan. After all, it was her fearless obedience to God that had brought him the French crown. But, in fact, he did nothing to help her during this time.

Joan was then taken to Rouen, the seat of the English occupation government, where she was put in chains in a castle dungeon to await trial. There, five male guards mocked and insulted her and made efforts to violate her. Fear of rape led Joan to continue wearing her masculine attire, which offered more protection than a dress.

In January 1431 it was announced that a church court would try Joan for heresy, blasphemy, and witchcraft. She pointed out that if this were the case, she ought to be held in a church prison and attended by nuns. But this ecclesiastical rule, like many others, was flouted.

Her trial began on January 9, 1431, and lasted five miserable months. The main judge in this sham court was Pierre Cauchon, whose appointment to this position was no coincidence. Cauchon despised Joan for humiliating him and damaging his career. Under his leadership as rector of the University of Paris, the university had thrown its support behind the Burgundians and developed the "double monarchy" theory—the idea that an English king should rule both England and France. But thanks to Joan, he and his theory were out of favor. Just before the coronation, he had been living in Reims. He was forced to flee from that city to Beavais. Then when that town welcomed Charles VII, he had to flee again. If during this trial Joan could be proved a heretic, Cauchon might have his revenge. He would see his "double monarchy" theory again viewed with the admiration it had once enjoyed.

Many witnesses were called in the trial, including bishops, abbots, and specialists in church law, but witnesses on Joan's behalf were not allowed to take part. Clerical notary Nicolas Bailly, commissioned to collect testimony against Joan, could find no adverse evidence, so legally speaking, there ought not to have been a trial at all. Her adversaries denied her the right to legal counsel and made certain that the tribunal sitting in judgment upon her was made up entirely of pro-English clergy. Documents were falsified, and any authorities who protested her treatment had their lives threatened. Such threats—and the domination of this trial by the secular English government—made the trial a mockery of justice. They were clear violations of the church's rules about such trials, which must be held without any interference from secular entities.

Still the trial took place, and it is one of the remarkable facts of history that the transcript of it survives. It reveals how bafflingly well this simple peasant girl performed against her highly educated, hostile English adversaries. Those who questioned her behaved much as attorneys do today, hoping to confuse her by jumping around in their questioning. They also repeated questions in an effort to get her to contradict herself. But to their chagrin and astonishment, she performed brilliantly.

At one point the members of the tribunal were so frustrated that they considered torturing Joan, but in the end they decided against it. In March she made a prediction, telling her goggle-eyed inquisitors,

"Within seven years the English will lose a greater prize than Orléans, and then, all France."[37] They hardly knew what to make of this, but she would be proved correct in 1450, when the English were finally driven from Paris and then lost the Battle of Formigny, in which they sacrificed some twenty-five hundred men—about 50 percent of their force. As a result, the French were able to retake much of their territory.

But Joan's most impressive moment came when she was asked a trick question: "Are you in a state of grace?" If she answered yes, she would have been charged with heresy, because the church taught that no one can know with certainty that he or she is in a state of grace. But if she answered no, it would be tantamount to acknowledging her own guilt. She cleverly replied, "If I am not, may God put me there; and if I am, may God so keep me."[38] According to a witness, her interrogators were astonished.

Joan also announced that her voices had told her that in three months she would be free. Whether she knew her freedom would come in the form of death we cannot know.

Exactly one year to the day of her capture, a priest arrived to exhort Joan "in loyalty to God . . . to accept authority and to submit."[39] It is possible he believed that Joan suffered from delusions and wished to save her from the terrible death that awaited her if she did not repent.

On May 14 Cauchon received a letter from the rector of the University of Paris to announce that, after various consultations and deliberations, they had reached unanimous consensus that the time had come to act. It declared that Joan was "an apostate, a liar, a schismatic, and a heretic."[40] Cauchon lost no time in sharing these conclusions with Joan's inquisitors. On May 23 they gave her their final and formal admonition.

Her reply was characteristically defiant and guileless. "If I were already judged and saw the fire lit," she said, "and the bundles of sticks ready and the executioners ready to light the fire, and even if I were within the fire, I would nevertheless not say anything other. I would maintain unto death what I have said in this trial."[41]

The following day Cauchon, intent on creating a dramatic spectacle, set up platforms in the abbey of Saint-Ouen's cemetery, one for Joan and additional ones for her judges. She was forced to listen to a sermon by the canon of Rouen, Guillaume Erard. Following the sermon, Erard ordered her: "Behold my Lords your Judges, who, at divers times, have summoned and required you to submit yourself, your words and deeds, to Our Holy Church, showing you that there did exist in your words and deeds many things which, as it did seem to the Clergy, are not good either to say or maintain."[42]

Joan was then handed a letter of abjuration, an oath of repudiation. Jean Massieu, an usher, urged her to sign it, so that her life might be spared. Twenty-five years later, Massieu reported it was clear to him that she did not seem to understand the document. The illiterate Maid asked that the letter "be inspected by the clerks, and that they should give her counsel." But Erard ordered Joan to sign the document immediately, "otherwise you will end your days by fire."[43]

And so, with the help of Laurence Calot, Joan signed the document by drawing a circle and a cross.

What did that document actually say, and what did Joan's peculiar "signature" signify? After all, she had signed documents before by writing her name. According to Pernoud and Clin, the document "was said to contain a promise that Joan would no longer wear men's clothes. According to the testimony of Guillaume Manchon, who in his capacity as a notary should have been aware of the meaning of this scene, Joan laughed. We may ask if the cross that she had just drawn in place of a signature . . . might not have been a reference to the cross she had sometimes put on military messages, as a previously agreed signal indicating that whoever received that letter should consider it null and void."[44]

The crowd of Englishmen were angry because their dearest wish—that Joan be condemned and executed—had not taken place. After serving a term as a heretic, she might well be allowed to return home. The Earl of Warwick complained, but Cauchon quietly reassured him: "My Lord, do not worry; we will catch her again."[45]

Afterward, Joan again asked to be placed into a church prison but was instead taken back to her dank castle cell. This decision was more crucial than it may appear. If convicted heretics relapsed, religious authorities could condemn them to death and hand them over to civil authorities, who would then carry out the sentence. As Pernoud and Clin explain, Cauchon "had succeeded only in making men's clothes the symbol of Joan's refusal to submit to the church."[46] She had promised not to wear them. But once back in her cell, she was again threatened with rape by her guards.

One witness said that three days later, she resumed wearing men's clothing, because they provided a better defense against sexual assault. Another witness said she resumed wearing them because her guards had removed her feminine clothing while she slept and thrown a bag filled with men's attire into her cell.

Regardless of the reason, when Cauchon discovered that Joan was once again wearing men's clothing, he quickly went to the castle prison. With him were Jean Lemaitre, the vice-inquisitor, and several others. Why, they demanded to know, had Joan resumed wearing men's clothing? She replied:

> I did it on my own will . . . because it was more lawful and convenient than to have women's clothes because I am with men; I began to wear them again because what was promised me was not observed, to wit that I should go to mass and receive the body of Christ and be freed from these irons. I would rather die than stay in these irons; but if it is permitted for me to go to mass, and if I could be freed of these irons, and if I could be put in a decent prison and if I could have a woman to help me, I would be good and do what the church wishes.[47]

Joan was then asked if she had heard from her voices. Yes, she replied; they had told her of God's "great sorrow that I did a very wicked thing to which I consented in abjuring and making a revocation, and said that I was damning myself to save my life."[48]

That was all Cauchon needed to hear. He left the prison, immediately went to the castle court, and told the Earl of Warwick: "Make good cheer. It is done."[49]

On May 30 two priests came to Joan and told her she would die at the stake that very morning. She burst into tears. When Cauchon visited her later, she lashed out at him, saying, "Bishop, it is by you that I die!"

The bishop condescendingly explained that Joan was to be executed because she did not keep her promise to refrain from wearing men's clothing. Enraged, Joan answered, "Had you put me in the Church's prison with women to guard me as was of right, this would not have been. I summon you before God the great Judge."[50]

Once more Cauchon violated procedural rules, which called for Joan to be taken to a hall where a secular bailiff could hear her case and pronounce a secular sentence. But he was taking no chances that she would escape the punishment he had marked out for her. Two hundred guards escorted her to the Old Marketplace, where the stake had been prepared atop a huge pile of wood. She was forced to wear a paper miter emblazoned with the words *"Heretique, Relapse, Apostat, Idolatre"* (Heretic, Relapsed, Apostate, Idolator).

The English soldiers helped her climb the wood piled around the stake and tied her to it with chains. She then asked for a cross. A sympathetic English soldier devised one of sticks and gave it to her. She kissed it and pushed it inside her clothing, and then she publicly forgave her enemies. Friar Isambart de la Pierre, intent on finding her a crucifix, located one in the Saint-Laurent church. But when he returned he saw that a torch already had been put to the wood beneath the Maid. As the flames crackled and Joan burned, he held the crucifix aloft so that she could look upon it.

According to witnesses, she continued "to praise God and the saints while lamenting devoutly; the last word she cried in a high voice as she died was: 'Jesus!'"[51]

Many in the English crowd that day—and there were hundreds—wept in pity for the girl. Joan's own cries deeply disturbed her executioner, who told a friar "that he had sinned gravely and that he repented what he had done against Joan, whom he now took to be a holy woman; for as it seemed to him, this Englishman had himself seen, at the moment that Joan gave up her spirit, a white dove emerge from her and take flight toward France."[52]

Jean Tressart, secretary to England's king, having seen Joan burn, lamented, "We are all ruined, for a good and holy person was burned."[53]

In order to prevent the collection of relics, English soldiers dug through the coals to expose her burned body. Concerned that people would claim that she had escaped death by fire, they then set fire to her body twice more; nothing now remained but ashes.

Her remains were then cast into the Seine. Thus ended the mortal life of Joan of Arc, the savior of France.

◆ ◆ ◆

But that is not the end of her story. In 1449, eighteen years after Joan's death, King Charles VII, along with Joan's mother and Inquisitor-General Jean Bréhal, asked Pope Callixtus III to authorize posthumously a "nullification trial" to determine whether Joan's original trial had been just, according to canon law. The pope agreed. Empaneled theologians called 115 witnesses and examined their testimony. In 1456 Bréhal issued a final summary. It was an utter repudiation of the previous verdict. Joan, he declared, was innocent. He further decreed that not only had she been killed unjustly but she had suffered a martyr's death.

Cauchon had Joan executed because she had supposedly violated biblical teachings about the proper clothing for men and women, but that conviction was reversed "in part because the condemnation proceeding had failed to consider the doctrinal exceptions to that stricture."[54]

But there was more to come. The vile Cauchon, who had convicted and executed the innocent Joan for personal reasons, was now himself denounced by the court as a heretic. It was poetic justice, marred only by the fact that Cauchon had died years before.

Nearly five hundred years after her death, in 1909, Joan of Arc was beatified; and in 1920, she was canonized as a saint in the Catholic Church.

TWO
Susanna Wesley

1669–1742

W hile writing my book about William Wilberforce,[1] I first came to appreciate the historic and cultural earthquake known as the Wesleyan Revival. Most of the dramatic social advances of the nineteenth century—including all that Wilberforce and his friend Hannah More were able to accomplish— were a direct result of that unprecedented outpouring of faith. It can be said without exaggeration that John and Charles Wesley's efforts— their evangelism and service to the poor, the disenfranchised, and the hopeless—changed the world. It also can be said without exaggeration that who these great men were and all they did in their lives had everything to do with the extraordinary woman who raised them.

◆ ◆ ◆

usanna Annesley Wesley came into the world in 1669, the twenty-fifth of twenty-five children born to her parents, the Rev. Samuel Annesley and his wife, Mary. Bitter religious controversies raged in England at that time. At the center of them all was the battle between the Church of England and the Puritans. King Charles I represented the Church of England, and Oliver Cromwell led the Puritans.

Having gained the upper hand in 1649, Cromwell and the Puritans had King Charles I imprisoned and then beheaded. Cromwell ruled England until his death in 1658, at which point the Royalists returned to power, making Charles I's son, Charles II, the new king. In 1662, in an attempt to wipe out Puritanism for good, Parliament passed the Act of Uniformity, decreeing that all religious leaders must follow the teachings of the Church of England.[2] But at the risk of their lives, two thousand ministers bravely refused to do this. One of them was Susanna's father, Samuel Annesley. As a result he lost his position, causing considerable hardship for his large family. In 1672, ten years after the act was passed, Charles II softened it, and most of the two thousand ministers immediately went back to their preaching.

Susanna Wesley was remarkably intelligent. While still a young girl her brilliant, curious mind absorbed and analyzed what was happening around her, especially since her own father and family were directly affected by it. Her childhood home was often filled with the intelligent and well-read friends of her father—including Daniel Defoe, the author of *Robinson Crusoe*—who vigorously debated theological issues. We don't know whether she attended a local school or was taught by older family members, but there can be little doubt she read many of the volumes in her father's library. Years later, as a mother teaching her own children, Susanna displayed, according to biographer Arnold A. Dallimore, "a theological knowledge superior to that of many ministers of that day."[3]

Given what her father suffered at the hands of the Royalists, it is quite remarkable that Susanna, at the age of twelve, made up her mind to become a member of the Church of England. Perhaps more remarkable yet is that her father gave her the liberty to do so. Her own account of her decision underscores her precocity. "Because I had been educated among the Dissenters," she wrote, "and there being something remarkable in my leaving them at so early an age, not being full thirteen, I had drawn up an account of the whole transaction, under which I included in the main of the controversy between them and the Established Church, as far as it had come to my knowledge."[4]

At her sister Elizabeth's wedding the following year, the brilliant thirteen-year-old met her future husband, nineteen-year-old Samuel Wesley. Samuel's father—another Dissenter—had died in prison, where he was serving time for preaching the Puritan way. Thanks to the generosity of his father's friends, Samuel had attended a Dissenting academy, where he focused on classical studies.

Despite his father's imprisonment and death at the hands of the established church, Samuel, like Susanna, had decided to join the Church of England. It's possible this was in part because he saw within the church's leadership structure a better chance of promotion through the ranks than with the Dissenters. In 1683 he began his studies at Oxford's Exeter College, supporting himself through publishing poetry, tutoring other students, and doing translations for Oxford's Bodleian Library. He took his bachelor of arts degree in 1688 and soon afterward was ordained and given a curacy, at which point he felt free to marry. He and Susanna had stayed in touch since their meeting six years earlier. They married on November 11, 1688. He was twenty-six, and she, nineteen.

Until their marriage, the couple had known each other almost exclusively through the letters they exchanged, but after they were married, they discovered to their dismay that, beyond their shared enthusiasm for the Church of England, they had less in common with each other than they might have hoped. One other thing they did have in common was a certain stubbornness, which would cause them difficulties in the years ahead.

Samuel could be impulsive too. For example, he had been in his curacy for only a few months when he decided to accept a position as a chaplain aboard a navy ship. It was true that the position offered more than twice what he had made as a curate, but a few months after the chaplaincy had begun, he gave that up as well, claiming he was mistreated and that the food was terrible. Things got so bad financially that Susanna, who was now pregnant, was obliged to live in a boarding house until he returned, after which they went to stay with her parents to await the baby's arrival.

On February 10, 1690, Susanna gave birth to the couple's first son, Samuel. The new father again found work as a curate and supplemented his meager pay with writing. But the rector of the church disapproved of his curate doing other work and promptly fired him. So the small family returned to the boarding house. Samuel was then offered a position as rector of St. Leonard's Church, located on the Isle of Axholme, a river-island in the northwest corner of Lincolnshire. He accepted the post, again supplementing his income with literary endeavors.

He soon found himself indebted to a number of people from whom he had borrowed money to furnish the rectory and to purchase farming implements. Sadly, the interest on and repayment of these sums would remain a burden for the remainder of his life.

More children followed in quick succession. A girl, named Susanna for her mother, was born in 1694; another daughter, Emelia, was born within the year but died some months after. In 1695 the Wesleys lost twin boys, who were just a few weeks old.

Susanna's father, Samuel Annesley, died in 1696, and for reasons no one can know, he left all his money to his other children. It is likely this was due in part to her decision to become a member of the Church of England. Nevertheless, she grieved greatly for her father.

Three more daughters—Susanna (nicknamed Sukey), Mary, and Mehetabel (nicknamed Hetty)—were born, followed by another set of twins, a boy and a girl, who both died shortly after their birth in 1701.

Daughters Anne and Martha followed a few years later, while John and Charles, brothers whose world-changing ministry would carry the Wesley name into the history books, came into the world in 1703 and 1707.

In 1697, following the death of King James II, William and Mary arrived from Holland to rule as king and queen of England. (Mary was King James's daughter.) Samuel Wesley had dedicated his book, *Life of Christ*, to her, and he now found himself invited by King William himself to become rector of a parish in Epworth, which paid far more than what he was receiving at St. Leonard's. So the family promptly packed up and moved to the three-story rectory. Epworth was located in a rural backwater about as remote from civilization and its benefits as one can imagine.

Writing to her brother, Susanna laments that this was hardly the ideal situation for the erudite man of letters who was her husband: "And did I not know that Almighty Wisdom hath views and ends in fixing the bounds of our habitation, which are out of our ken, I should think it a thousand pities that a man of his brightness and rare endowments of learning and useful knowledge in relation to the church of God should be confined to an obscure corner of the country, where his talents are buried, and he determined to a way of life for which he is not so well qualified as I could wish."[5]

◆ ◆ ◆

But the distance from literary society was not the principal difficulty. Not long after moving to Epworth, Samuel Wesley's renown had the odd result of adding to the family's growing debts. He was invited to preach the Visitation Sermon in Gainsborough and to speak before the Society for the Reformation of Manners. These were great honors, but the humble man of God was expected to pay his own traveling expenses. In addition his position as a proctor of the Lincoln diocese was also unpaid.

Samuel decided to try his hand at farming to supplement his

income. He worked hard, but still the debts increased. In 1700 Samuel appealed to the Archbishop of York, Dr. John Sharpe, listing all his expenses—including rebuilding a barn and supporting his elderly mother—which had led to his falling three hundred pounds into debt, an astounding sum, considering his annual salary was just two hundred pounds. The archbishop was moved to help Samuel financially and even prevailed upon others to do so. But his financial difficulties continued. He was overwhelmed by it all, especially given the increasing number of children he had to support. He fell into a depression, terribly disappointed that he had not made more of a success of his life.

It was during this time that he made a desperate and irresponsible decision: he abandoned his wife, his children, and his congregation. The reason he gave for leaving had nothing to do with his finances. Many years later, his son John described the grim situation: "The year before King William died my father observed my mother did not say amen to the prayer for the king. She said she could not, for she did not believe that the Prince of Orange was king. He vowed he would not cohabit with her till she did. He then took horse and rode away; nor did she hear anything of him for a twelvemonth."[6]

Susanna was hardly alone in refusing to view King William III, Prince of Orange—who was Dutch—as England's true king. Many shared her view. King William's claim to the throne came through his wife, Queen Mary II. She was the daughter of James II, and she and William served as co-regents of England, Scotland, and Ireland while James was exiled during the religious wars. They were crowned in 1689. But it's hard for us to fathom how something like this could cause such problems in the Wesley marriage.

Precisely why Susanna wouldn't mutter an "amen" to assuage her distressed and sensitive husband's feelings, or conversely why something so seemingly small could be the excuse for a man to abandon his family, causing them to suffer tremendously, is a great mystery to us, three centuries hence. Here is a window into Susanna's thinking in a letter to her friend, Lady Yarborough.

> You advise me to continue with my husband, and God knows how gladly I would do it, but there, there is my supreme affliction, he will not live with me. . . . [Since] I'm willing to let him quietly enjoy his opinions, he ought not to deprive me of my little liberty of conscience.[7]

Susanna also confided in Suffragan Bishop George Hickes:

> My master will not be persuaded he has no power over the conscience of his Wife. . . . He is now for referring the whole to the Archbishop of York and Bishop of Lincoln, and says if I will not be determined by them, he will do anything rather than live with a person that is the declared enemy of his country.[8]

After Samuel had been absent for a year, however, fate intervened. The house in which Susanna and her children were living caught fire, nearly killing one of her small daughters and destroying most of the house and all their belongings. Upon hearing this news, Samuel returned to his family and set about rebuilding the house. And since Queen Anne had ascended the English throne during this time, the Dutch-born source of the couple's conflict had been removed.

◆ ◆ ◆

As her husband rebuilt their home, Susanna turned her attention to the education of her children, a job she would continue for twenty years as additional offspring arrived. It was not at all customary to educate girls in that time, so it is remarkable that Susanna wanted not just her three sons, but all her children to be able to read, write, and reason well. Nor did her ideas about education end with letters and logic. She also knew that above all she must teach her children to love God.

As far as she was concerned, the state of their souls formed the focus of her education. Much of what she taught them was for the purpose of helping them see through—and therefore be able to resist—the secular doctrines of that time. So she may be regarded not only as the inventor of homeschooling, but also of what today is sometimes called "worldview teaching," something modern Christian parents in the West have begun embracing as they raise their children in an increasingly post-Christian culture.

Susanna's dedication to educating her children is simply staggering. "Though the education of so many children must create abundance of trouble," she wrote,

> and will perpetually keep the mind employed as well as the body; yet consider 'tis no small honour to be entrusted with the care of so many souls. . . . [I]t will be certainly no little accession to the future glory to stand forth at the last day and say, "Lord, here are the children which Thou hast given me, of whom I have lost none by my ill example, nor by neglecting to instill in their minds, in their early years, the principles of Thy true religion and virtue!"[9]

Each child's formal education began at age five, but much earlier than that, Susanna taught them that there "was a Supreme Being to whom their gratitude and homage must be reverently rendered."[10] She taught them to treat both their siblings and the servants with great courtesy. Even before they could walk or talk, they were "taught to ask a blessing upon their food by appropriate signs; thus learning, at the very beginning, to recognize their dependence upon" God.[11] Susanna helped them memorize short prayers and had them say the Lord's Prayer upon rising and retiring.

When Susanna failed to find textbooks that met her exacting standards, she decided to write her own. The first textbook took on arguments about the nature of the universe and how it pointed to God as the creator. The book invited her children to use reason and intellect to evaluate the teachings of their faith critically. She wanted to equip them with the tools to analyze the objections to faith that were so prevalent in the "Age of Reason."

Susanna's second textbook was her own exposition of the Apostles' Creed. A remarkably sophisticated piece of writing, the book is written simply enough for children to understand. Her third explored the teachings of the Ten Commandments, which she used to teach her children the fundamentals of divine moral law and to show that God's moral law was universal, for all human beings in all times.

Clearly, Susanna could not have taught her children so well had she herself not been encouraged as a child to read deeply, to listen to the debates of her elders, and to join in theological conversations.

The children's daily routine was rigorous. Susanna required them to study for three hours each morning and three each afternoon, six days a week. They began and closed each academic day by singing a psalm and reading from the Bible. Most of her children learned the entire alphabet on their first day of school. Discipline was the order of the day, which the children were accustomed to. They had been subjected to Susanna's notions of discipline from birth.

The "Mother of Methodism," as she was called later, was manifestly methodical in raising her children. Her babies were fed on a schedule, rather than being fed on demand, as is the preferred method today. But that was just the beginning. "The children were always put into a regular method of living," she wrote, "in such things as they were capable of, from their birth; as in dressing and undressing, changing their linen, etc. . . ." When they turned a year old (and some before) they were taught "to fear the rod."[12] To raise them otherwise, she felt, would have been selfish and cruel. "[B]y this means," she wrote, "they escaped abundance of correction they might otherwise have had."[13]

She was not strict for its own sake. "In the esteem of the world," she wrote, "they pass for kind and indulgent, whom I call cruel, parents, who permit their children to get habits which they know must be afterward broken."[14]

Her belief that girls should be educated ran so deep that she refused to teach her daughters to work until they could first read excellently. She said that parents who did not enforce this rule were "the very reason why so few women can read fit to be heard."[15]

After her small children finished their supper and had their baths, they were put to bed awake, "for there was no such thing allowed of in our house as sitting by a child until it fell asleep."[16] Of course, this sounds much less harsh when we remember how many children she had to bring up.

"When the will of a child is totally subdued, and it is brought to revere and stand in awe of the parents," she wrote in a letter to her son John, "then a great many childish follies, and inadvertencies may be passed by. Some should be overlooked and taken no notice of, and others mildly reproved; no willful transgression ought ever to be forgiven children, without chastisement, less or more, as the nature and circumstances of the offense require."[17]

So "childish follies" could be overlooked, but not willful disobedience. In the same letter to John, Susanna explained the spiritual basis for all this discipline: "I insist upon conquering the will of children betimes [early] because this is the only strong and rational foundation of a religious education, without which both precept and example will be ineffectual. But when this is thoroughly done, then a child is capable of being governed by the reason and piety of its parents till its own understanding comes to maturity, and the principles of religion have taken root in the mind."[18]

No one can doubt that Susanna's methods of child rearing resulted in children who grew to show tremendous strength of character. And strict attention to the children's behavior meant that "taking God's name in vain, cursing and swearing, profanity, obscenity, rude ill-bred names, were never heard among them."[19] While her children did their schoolwork, Susanna sewed, went over household accounts, wrote letters, and nursed the latest baby. At night before bed the children played games, sang psalms, and read books from their father's library. Samuel Wesley also took part in educating his children, teaching his sons Greek, Latin, and classical literature in order to prepare them for additional, formal schooling at boarding schools, to which all of the boys were subsequently sent.

One of the most dramatic examples of how busy and crowded the house often was is that as a signal to her children to be quiet, Susanna would sometimes sit down and pull her apron over her head so that she could pray in peace. When she was thus accoutered, the children knew not to interrupt her.

❖ ❖ ❖

In 1705, something else happened that would add to the family's woes. During an election campaign, Samuel came out in support of two of the four men running—one Tory and one Whig. But when he discovered that the Whig position on the church and royalty differed from his own, he withdrew his support, causing the Whig candidate's supporters to publicly attack Samuel. And then the real troubles began. Samuel wrote a letter about it to Archbishop Sharpe.

"The election began on Wednesday, 30th," he wrote. "A great part of the night our Isle people kept drumming, shouting, and firing of pistols and guns under the window where my wife lay, who had been brought to bed [to recover from childbearing] not three weeks. I had put the child to nurse [the nurse lived nearby]; . . . the noise kept his nurse waking till one or two in the morning. Then they left off, and the nurse, being heavy to sleep, overlaid the child," suffocating him.[20] Frightened servants threw the dead child into the arms of a barely awake Susanna.

What this must have been like for her can only be imagined. Later, Samuel was told by friends that some of the local men intended to kill him. When he arrived home, "they sent the drum and mob, with guns etc., to compliment me till after midnight. One of them, passing by on Friday evening and seeing my children in the yard cried out, 'O ye devils! We will come and turn ye all out of doors a-begging shortly.'"[21]

The vicious harassment continued for some time, and what they suffered seems unimaginable. Villagers stabbed several of the family's cattle, wounded their dog, and set fire to their crops. Then one of the men to whom Samuel was indebted, furious over his change of mind in the election, had Samuel tossed into debtors' prison, where he languished for some time. At one point, Susanna sent him her wedding rings so that he might sell them and pay off his debt, but he would not hear of it and sent the rings back.

Of course, with Samuel behind bars, Susanna found it more difficult than ever to feed her large family. The vile characters behind such attacks were attempting "to starve my poor family in my absence," Samuel wrote, "my cows being all dried up by it, which was their chief subsistence,"[22] because the cows provided milk, butter, and cheese for the Wesleys. Friends eventually sent enough money to pay off Samuel's debt, allowing him to return home, where he bravely continued his parish work.

But in 1709 the most terrifying event yet to affect the Wesley family took place when the family's home burned a second time. Susanna described the event to her nineteen-year-old son, Samuel, then away at school:

The fire broke out about eleven or twelve o'clock, we being all in bed, nor did we perceive it till the roof of the corn chamber . . . fell upon your sister Hetty's bed. . . .

We had no time to take our clothes. . . . When I was in the yard I looked about for your father and the children; but seeing none, concluded 'em all lost. But thank God, I was mistaken! Your father carried sister Emily, Suky, and Patty into the garden; then, missing Jacky [John], he ran back into the house, to see if he could save him. He heard him miserably crying out in the nursery and attempted several times to get upstairs, but was beat back by the flame; then he thought him lost and commended his soul to God and went to look after the rest. The child climbed up to the window, and called out to them in the yard; they got up to the casement and pulled him out just as the roof fell into the chamber.[23]

Another servant, Harry, saved Mary and Hetty by breaking the glass in the parlor window and throwing them out to safety.

This time the house burned to the ground completely, along with everything they owned. Having suffered thus twice, Samuel would now rebuild the house with brick. It is certainly possible that Samuel's enemies started the fire. In any event the terrifying event was life-altering and contributed to Susanna's many difficulties. As she wrote to her brother years later, "Mr. Wesley rebuilt his house in less than a year; but nearly thirteen years are elapsed since it was burned, yet it is not half furnished, nor his wife and children half clothed to this day."[24]

A month after the fire, Samuel and Susanna's nineteenth and last child, Kezia, came into the world. Nine of the Wesley children had died in infancy; those who survived were three sons—Samuel, John, and Charles—and seven daughters: Emelia, Susanna, Mary, Hetty, Anne, Martha, and Kezia.

◆ ◆ ◆

The fire not only threatened the lives of the Wesley children but also had an adverse effect on their characters as well and, Susanna feared, their very souls. During the many months it took to rebuild the rectory, the children lived in the homes of friends and relatives as far away as London. Susanna lamented: "Never were children better disposed to piety . . . till that fatal dispersion of them, after the fire, into several families. In those they were left at full liberty . . . to run abroad, and play with any children, good or bad. They soon learned to neglect a strict observation of the Sabbath, and got knowledge of several songs and bad things. . . . A clownish accent, and many rude ways, were learned, which were not reformed without some difficulty."[25]

When the children were finally home again, Susanna supplemented the classroom teaching with weekly visits with each child, helping them to understand how wicked their new habits were and how to behave in a way more pleasing to God, not to mention their parents.

The highly organized way Susanna reared and educated her children had the strongest influence on her son, John. In fact, while studying at Oxford he was mocked by other students for the highly organized way he approached the practice of his faith. He led a club of Oxford students who assiduously prayed, fasted, and performed acts of charity. Because their fellow students thought them so especially methodical, they took to calling the group he formed the "Methodists." John decided to take this insulting term as a compliment, adopting it with pride. It eventually became the name of the movement that swept first across England and then across the American colonies, changing the world in ways that are still felt today, more than two centuries later.

◆ ◆ ◆

Susanna's influence extended well beyond her own children. In 1712 a curate named Inman came to assist Samuel, so on the Sundays that Samuel was out of town, Inman preached the sermon. He had a mysterious predilection for preaching on the evils of debt, which the congregation did not find terribly compelling. Susanna was displeased that her children were not getting better spiritual food, so she decided to gather them in the kitchen each Sunday afternoon and read aloud printed sermons that her father or husband had written.

At first only her children and the servants were present, but soon others began to ask if they could attend. Before long the house was crammed with scores of people wanting to hear Susanna read the sermons—more people than were attending church each week. In fact, the morning church services eventually dwindled to almost nothing. Whenever Inman was preaching, most parishioners skipped church in the morning and showed up at the Wesley home in the afternoon.

Inman was predictably outraged and promptly fired off a letter to

Samuel in London, accusing Susanna of conducting an "illegal meeting." Samuel then wrote his wife, suggesting she allow a man to read the sermons aloud, inasmuch as it was then considered improper for women to preach. But she responded that few if any of her listeners could read well enough to carry out the project. Nor was she actually preaching, but only reading.

When Samuel persisted in criticizing her, she erupted with the righteous exactitude for which she was so well-known: "If you do, after all, think fit to dissolve this assembly, do not tell me that you desire me to do it, for that will not satisfy my conscience; but send me your positive command, in such full and express terms, as may absolve me from guilt and punishment for neglecting this opportunity of doing good, when you and I shall appear before the great and awful tribunal of our Lord Jesus Christ."[26]

Samuel was not willing to go that far, and the Sunday afternoon sermon reading continued. When he returned home, he discovered that, thanks to his wife's "illegal" efforts, his congregation had swelled considerably, and relations between the Wesleys and their neighbors were greatly improved.

◆ ◆ ◆

Susanna rarely failed to keep her evening appointment with God. Her fierce commitment to a fixed schedule, especially in her devotional life, is what we would expect from the "Mother of Methodism," but sometimes it is almost comical in its impressiveness. "For many years," her son John wrote, "my mother was employed in an abundance of temporal business. Yet she never suffered anything to break in upon her stated hours of retirement, which she sacredly observed from the age of 17 or 18 to 72."[27]

Susanna's devotional writings give us an insight into her piety, as well as into the varying and seemingly constant difficulties she faced. Like many busy wives and mothers, she appears sometimes to have felt overwhelmed. "O God, I find it most difficult to preserve a devout and serious temper of mind in the midst of much worldly business," she wrote. "Were I permitted to choose a state of life, or positively to ask of Thee anything in this world, I would humbly choose and beg that I might be placed in such a station wherein I might have daily bread with moderate care and that I might have more leisure to retire from the world without injuring those dependent on me."[28]

The woman who twice endured the loss of her home by fire wrote: "Help me, O Lord, to make a true use of all disappointments and calamities in this life, in such a way that they may unite my heart more closely with thee."[29]

In her difficulties, she was likely tempted to be jealous of her neighbors. She sought guidance in this matter as well: "May I give way to no direct murmurings, no repinings at the prosperity of others. . . . Save me from thinking severely or unjustly of others: from being too much dejected or disposed to peevishness, covetousness, or negligence in affairs."[30]

Spending twenty years teaching her children at home may have led to loneliness too. She wrote, "Enable me to live so as to deserve a friend, and if I never have one on earth, be Thou my friend, for in having Thee I shall have all that is dear and valuable in friendship."[31]

The persistent financial difficulties must have been especially hard to bear, and she wrote prayers asking for help in learning to accept them: "May I learn by practice to love Thee above all things, that so I may be out of the power of the world and my earthly circumstances give me no uneasiness, I would have my wealth to be Thy favor."[32]

If life was not difficult enough for Susanna, bizarre supernatural events began taking place at the Epworth rectory. They began on a cold December night in 1715: odd knockings with no discoverable source; the distinct sound of footsteps going up and down stairs;

sudden winds blowing *inside* the house; doors flying open of their own accord; and mysterious shrieks in the night. The family hardly knew what to make of it. Had demonic forces been assigned to frustrate the work of these diligent servants of God?

The first to experience the strange happenings was a maid named Nanny Marshal, who told the family of hearing sounds "like the dismal groans of a man in the pains of dying." Then one by one, Sukey, Anne, Emelia, and a young servant boy began noticing strange noises as well.

Susanna assumed that rats were responsible for the noises, until one night she went into her daughter Emelia's room and heard strange noises coming from beneath the bed. Suddenly, a small animal, which the eminently sober-thinking Susanna said she thought to be a "headless badger,"[33] ran across the room and then disappeared.

In the superstition of that day, a ghost often portended a death in the family, so Susanna told Samuel what was going on. Samuel himself believed in ghosts and apparitions but adamantly refused to believe his own house was being haunted. "Sukey," he told his wife sternly, "I am ashamed of you. These boys and girls frighten one another; but you are a woman of sense and should know better. Let me hear of it no more."[34]

But he would hear of it again, and not from his wife. One night Samuel himself was awakened by the sound of knocks. Some nights later the knocks returned, this time so loud the Wesleys were unable to sleep. Samuel and Susanna searched the house together but kept hearing sounds that seemed to emanate from the room they had just inspected. Samuel actually wondered whether his daughters or their male admirers might be playing tricks on the family.

But after he invited another minister, Joseph Hoole, to witness the disturbances, he changed his mind. Walking through the house that night, both men heard the strange tappings and saw Samuel's daughters trembling in their beds. Angered, Samuel prepared to shoot a pistol in the direction of the noises, stopping only when Hoole reminded him that no earthly missile could harm a spirit.

The irritated Samuel finally threw out a challenge: "Thou deaf and dumb devil, why doest thou frighten children that cannot answer thee? Come to me in my study that am a man!"[35]

On Christmas Day, the spirit made its presence known to the entire family. As Susanna later wrote, "There was such a noise in the room over our heads, as if several people were walking, then running up and down stairs . . . that we thought the children would be frightened." As she and Samuel searched the house, the spirit kept up its "rattling and thundering in every room, and even blowing an invisible horn at deafening decibels."[36]

For nearly a month following this yuletide cacophony, the family heard nothing. But then the spirit returned with a vengeance. During their evening devotion, the family heard knocks as they prayed for the king, and upon reaching the "amen," they heard a load thump. The spirit seemed to delight in harassing Samuel. As daughter Susanna wrote to her brother Samuel, "Last Sunday, to my father's no small amazement, his trencher [wooden plate] danced upon the table a pretty while, without anybody's stirring the table."[37] The spirit also pushed Samuel forcefully against his desk several times.

When concerned clergymen friends urged Samuel to abandon the rectory, he answered, "No; let the devil flee from me; I will not flee from him."[38]

The antics of the spirit stopped abruptly in early February 1716, three months after they had begun. With the single exception of Hetty, every one of the Wesleys living at the rectory when the spirit made his presence known wrote about their experiences. Susanna described the strange events in a letter to her son John, then away at the Charterhouse School in London, and tried to determine just why the apparition had appeared:

> I do not doubt the fact, but I cannot understand why these apparitions are permitted. If they were allowed to speak to us, and we had strength to bear such converse, if they had commission to inform us

of anything relating to their invisible world that would be of any use to us in this, if they would instruct us how to avoid danger, or put us in a way of being wiser and better, there would be sense in it; but to appear for no end that we know of, unless to frighten people almost out of their wits, seems altogether unreasonable.[39]

Given the theological sophistication of Susanna, it is odd that demonic disturbance did not occur to her as the simplest explanation.

◆ ◆ ◆

With her sons away at London schools, Susanna continued teaching them in the form of long letters. She took particular pains to warn them of the temptations common to young men away from home for the first time. Regarding the consumption of alcoholic beverages, Susanna warned Samuel, "Two glasses cannot hurt you, provided they contain no more than those commonly used. . . . Have a care; stay at the third glass; I consider you have an obligation to strict temperance, which all have not—I mean your designation for holy orders."[40] She also wrote to John about "the dangers of human love" and passion.[41]

Samuel wrote his sons too. One letter in particular reveals that he had learned to value his wife:

You know what you owe to one of the best of mothers . . . often reflect on the tender and peculiar love your dear mother has always expressed towards you, the deep affliction both of body and mind which she underwent for you both before and after your birth; the particular care she took of your education when she struggled with so many pains and infirmities; and, above all, the wholesome and sweet motherly advice and counsel which she has often given you to fear God, to take care of your soul, as well as your learning, to shun all vicious practices and bad examples. . . . You will not forget to evidence this by supporting and comforting her in her age. . . . In short, reverence and love her as much as you will.[42]

Given such kind words, Samuel's behavior toward his wife is puzzling. By all accounts, he allowed her and his daughters to live in poverty, spending whatever money he had on the best education that England had to offer for his three sons. When his own brother, Matthew, condemned him for this, Samuel's response was that God would take care of his family after he was gone. For her part, Susanna—and her children—shared Matthew's view that they were being forced to suffer because of Samuel's poor financial decisions. One daughter later wrote feelingly on the "scandalous want of necessaries,"[43] blaming them for the many illnesses her mother suffered.

The growing Wesley daughters were now attracting the attention of young men. They lived in the hope that Susanna's brother, Samuel Annesley, who had made a fortune in India, would soon return and keep a promise he had made to help his nieces financially. The family was still quite poor, and the girls had to help take care of the farm animals and assist with the housework. Daughter Emelia worked as a teacher in Lincoln, some distance from home.

Annesley wrote his brother-in-law, asking if he would like to manage his business affairs in London. Susanna expressed doubts about her husband's ability to do so, but Samuel took the job and in short order proved his wife's judgment correct. His annoyed brother-in-law fired him and announced that he was now having second thoughts about assisting the Wesley daughters as he had promised. Once again, Samuel Wesley's actions had spoiled things.

This was a crushing disappointment to the girls—so much so that in 1721, Sukey felt compelled to rush into marriage with a wealthy man of base character named Richard Ellison. Susanna upbraided her brother for Sukey's unhappiness, writing, "When, by your last unkind letters, she perceived that all her hopes in you were frustrated, rashly threw herself upon a man (if a man he maybe called who is little inferior to the apostate angels in wickedness) that is not only her plague, but a constant affliction to the family."[44] Years later, Sukey left her husband to live with her four grown children.

Susanna also gave a lively defense of her husband, whom Annesley had apparently accused of dishonesty. Brother and sister apparently made up their quarrel, and when Annesley returned to England, Susanna traveled to London to watch his ship dock. But to her great dismay and bafflement, her brother was not on the boat, though his possessions were. The ship's crew did not know what had happened to him: Had he fallen overboard, or had he been murdered and his body thrown to the sharks? His loss was a heavy burden for Susanna to bear. But even worse was to come.

Perhaps the brightest, loveliest, and liveliest of Susanna's daughters was auburn-haired Hetty. Following the fire that destroyed her home, Hetty, then aged twelve, and her fourteen-year-old sister, Sukey, were sent to live in London with their uncle Matthew, a well-to-do doctor and apothecary, and his wife for more than a year. In London the girls not only had the freedom they did not enjoy at home, but they also became accustomed to greater luxury and the entertainments London provided.

Once they returned home the girls were bored, and the shortage of eligible young suitors frustrated them. Whenever they did enjoy the company of young men, their father considered the men beneath his daughters. At the age of twenty-seven, Hetty was, as biographer Sir Arthur Quiller-Couch described her, "a queen in a country smock and cobbled shoes, a woman made for love, and growing toward love, though repressed and thwarted."[45]

Given the youthful age at which young women married in those days, it is curious that the beautiful Hetty, now approaching thirty, was still unmarried. Were the young men who courted her truly beneath her, or was her father behaving unwisely yet again by refusing to allow Hetty to find a mate? While Hetty loved her mother, she resented her father.

Her resentment surely increased when her father insisted she break off her romance with a young schoolteacher named John Romley. Samuel had become angry, and probably embarrassed, when Romley sang a song before a group of people that, according to Dallimore, "was a stinging parody of the changes made by Samuel Wesley in his endeavours to gain preferment."[46] An outraged Samuel ordered Romley out of his house, and told Hetty to have nothing more to do with him. Defiantly, Hetty secretly exchanged letters with Romley, and when her father discovered this, he sent Hetty to a nearby village to serve as a companion to a wealthy woman, Mrs. Grantham.

Not surprisingly Hetty hated her new life, and she soon left the position. It is not known where Hetty went or what she did in the months after leaving Mrs. Grantham, but some months later, she returned to the family home and, to her parents' horror, was five months pregnant.

Hetty hoped she might be allowed to marry the child's father, whom she loved, but Samuel would not hear of it. He had for some reason determined that Hetty should instead marry a journeyman plumber and glazier named William Wright, an illiterate man who lacked manners and was too fond of alcohol. The plumber was delighted to be given such a prize as the beautiful Hetty, but her mother, sisters, and brothers were outraged and could not fathom how Samuel could condemn his bright, educated daughter to such a fate.

Daughter Mary stood up to him, saying, "Oh, sir, you are a good man! But you are seldom kind and rarely just. . . . You are a tyrant to those you love, and now in your tyranny you are going to do what even in your tyranny you have never done before—a downright wickedness!"[47] Her brother John even preached a sermon, "Showing Charity to Sinners," before his father, hoping to get him to change his mind, but the stubborn Samuel became even more determined to proceed with his plans. Less than two weeks after her return home, Hetty was married to Wright, and the pair moved in with Wright's father, himself an unpleasant man.

The child arrived in February 1726 but soon died, and a devastated Hetty interpreted the loss of her child as a sign of God's judgment. Then, Hetty's uncle Matthew Annesley came to her rescue, giving the couple a gift of five hundred pounds, which allowed them to move to London and start a new business. After Hetty lost two more babies, her husband began drinking heavily, and Uncle Matthew again took pity on her, taking her to Bristol for a break, where she could meet people of her own kind. In time, Susanna forgave her daughter the great shame she had brought to the family, and the two became close. But Hetty's father never forgave her.

In 1749, twenty-four years after her forced marriage, fifty-two-year-old Hetty began not only attending her brother John's religious services in London, but also actively assisting him. She died in 1753 at the age of fifty-five.

Several other of the Wesley children also endured unhappy marriages. Emelia twice fell in love, but both times her brothers advised her against marrying the man—one, because his character was not what they felt it should be, and the other because he was a Quaker. Now in her forties, two decades beyond the age at which women married at that time, Emelia made a desperate choice. She married an apothecary who was a bad businessman and who took whatever money Emelia made from her work at a school for girls. The man proved to be heartless and by all accounts made Emelia's life miserable.

Martha fell in love with Westley Hall, a clergyman who proved to be of ignoble character. Soon after their engagement, he met Martha's younger sister Kezia, who knew nothing of the engagement, and his ardent attentions caused Kezia to fall in love with him. Eventually, Hall claimed that God had told him to go back to Martha, and the couple were wed. Some years later, Hall seduced a young seamstress, who became pregnant, and afterward fathered a second illegitimate child. Eventually he declared himself an atheist and abandoned Martha altogether.

Not all the sisters married unhappily. Anne married John Lambert, a land surveyor, and the marriage turned out well; and Mary, at the advanced age of thirty-eight, wed a curate. The couple was very happy, but Mary died in childbirth before the pair had celebrated their first anniversary. She was the first of three adult children Susanna would lose.

Kezia, the youngest and most delicate daughter, seems never to have recovered from having her heart broken by Westley Hall. She died when she was just thirty-two.

As for the Wesley brothers, John jumped impulsively—though he was forty-eight—into marriage with a widow named Mary Vazeille. The couple was deeply unhappy, and when after fifteen years his wife left, the great man confided to his journal, "I did not forsake her, I did not dismiss her, I will not recall her."[48]

Charles was happily married to Sarah Gwynne, and Samuel was happily married to Ursala Berry, the daughter of a vicar. To Susanna's great grief, Samuel, her favorite child, died in 1739, aged forty-nine.

◆ ◆ ◆

B y the time her son John was ordained a deacon in 1725, Susanna was fifty-six, and she and Samuel were beginning to suffer the symptoms of old age. Samuel had a stroke that left him with a paralyzed right hand. Unable to write, he made use of his daughters for both his correspondence and a commentary he was writing on the book of Job. That their arduous life might have given him something to say on the subject is no surprise. Susanna, who had over the years suffered episodes of gout and rheumatism, now had what her husband described in a letter to John and Charles as "little convulsions."[49]

After surviving several accidents Samuel was ill for six months and then died in April 1735. He was seventy-three, and predictably he left behind numerous and significant debts.

And inasmuch as the vicarage must now be vacated for the new vicar, Susanna found herself again homeless. Worse yet, those to whom Samuel owed money now put pressure on her, in one case even having her arrested. Her sons quickly stepped forward with financial help, and Susanna moved in with daughter Emelia, who lived at the school where she was employed. John and Charles had at this time decided to sail to America as missionaries, leaving their mother with no notion of when they would return. Susanna afterward went to live with her oldest son, Samuel, and his wife and then one year later to the home of her daughter Martha and her husband, Westley Hall. This was of course before Hall abandoned his wife.

After John and Charles returned from America, they famously underwent a great spiritual transformation when they heard their friend the evangelist George Whitefield preach the electrifying message: "You must be born again." For them, it would change everything. The pair also came in contact with evangelical Moravians, from whom they understood that although one must indeed work out one's salvation "with fear and trembling," salvation was nonetheless not by one's good works, but by faith. At a Moravian meeting in London on May 24, 1738, John heard a reading of Martin Luther's preface to the Epistle to the Romans. It was after this that he penned his now famous words: "I felt my heart strangely warmed."[50]

Just a few weeks later he preached a sermon on the subject of salvation by faith and soon thereafter preached another sermon on the doctrine of grace, which he described as "free in all, and free for all."[51]

Charles also experienced this new understanding of salvation. It happened three days before his brother's conversion, on May 21, 1738. This led him to write his famous hymn, "And Can It Be." It is one of the most popular of the six thousand he wrote.

The Wesley brothers shared their views with their mother, who had taught her children, as she put it in a letter to Samuel when he was a teenager, to "carefully 'work out your salvation with fear and trembling,' lest you should finally miscarry."[52]

In another letter to Charles, Susanna wrote, "Blessed be God, who showed you the necessity you were in of a Savior to deliver you from the power of sin and Satan (for Christ will be no Saviour to such as see not their need of one), and directed you by faith to lay hold of that stupendous mercy offered us by redeeming love. . . . Blessed be God, he is an all-sufficient Saviour; and blessed be his holy name that thou hast found him a Savior to thee, my son!"[53]

In 1739 Susanna went to live with her son John, who had purchased a building called the Foundry. While most of it was converted into meeting space, John turned a portion of it into an apartment for himself and his mother, where she was able to live comfortably for the final three years of her life. In a communion service at the Foundry in 1740, Susanna for some reason found herself deeply affected by the words from *The Book of Common Prayer*, "The blood of our Lord Jesus Christ which was given for me." "These words struck through my heart," she wrote, "and I knew that God for Christ's sake had forgiven me all my sins."[54]

In 1742, Susanna, now aged seventy-three, began to fail. Her remaining five daughters—Susanna, Anne, Emelia, Hetty, and Martha—and John and Charles—gathered around her. Charles was forced to leave but hoped his mother would linger until his return. On July 20, John wrote, "I found my mother on the borders of eternity; but she has no doubt or fear, nor any desire but (as soon as God should call) 'to depart and be with Christ.'"[55] Susanna died the following day. But according to her children, who witnessed it, she awoke twelve hours before her death, and declared: "My dear Saviour! Are you come to help me in my extremity at last?"[56] As Susanna had requested, her children, to whom she had devoted so much of her time, energy, and love, sang a psalm of praise to God at her death.

Few human beings have influenced the world as Susanna Wesley did. The manner in which she taught her children greatly influenced the work of her son, John, and the Methodist movement he founded led to world-changing revival and to such an array of social reforms as can never be calculated. The abolition of the slave trade and slavery are at the top of a long list that includes penal reform, the end of child labor in England, laws against cruelty to animals, and the establishment of countless private societies and organizations dedicated to caring for the poor and suffering. The denomination he founded today claims eighty million members around the world, along with many Methodist hospitals, colleges, and orphanages.

More than 375 years after her death, we sing the hymns Susanna's son Charles wrote—including "Hark! The Herald Angels Sing," the Easter hymn "Christ the Lord Is Risen Today," and the Christmas song "Come Thou Long Expected Jesus." Despite tremendous trials, each of Susanna's children passionately embraced faith in God and lived out that faith to the end of their days.

Anyone believing that the life of a woman dedicated to her family must be less than optimal cannot know the story of Susanna Wesley. Despite poverty, illness, a difficult marriage, and heartbreak in endless forms, she used her intellect, creativity, time, energies, and will in such a way that can hardly be reckoned. The world in which we live owes much of the goodness in it to her life.

THREE
Hannah More

1745–1833

O ne of the great joys of writing *Amazing Grace: William Wilberforce and the Heroic Campaign to End Slavery* was that in learning about the extraordinary Wilberforce I also got to know a number of his brilliant and eccentric friends, Granville Sharp[1] and Isaac Milner[2] being two of the most colorful. But the third figure in the superlative triumvirate of geniuses I discovered while researching Wilberforce was the incomparable Hannah More.

More was nothing less than the most influential woman of her time. She was already a well-known figure when Wilberforce met her in 1787: a best-selling playwright and author, whose works at the time outsold Jane Austen's ten to one, and a woman of such boundless wit and charm that everyone wished to be in her society. She was close with Samuel Johnson, David Garrick, Horace Walpole, and every other bold-faced name of that day, but it was her friendship with Wilberforce that fueled their collaborations against the slave trade and a host of other social evils. Between them, they would quite literally change the world.

When I stumbled across Hannah More, I almost could not believe she existed. It was as though I had discovered a gurgling Bernini fountain in the midst of a desert. When I came to fathom the crucial role she played in the history of abolition and the so-called Reformation of Manners, I was positively disturbed at the outrageous ellipsis. So to remedy it in the tiniest way, I crammed all I could about her into my Wilberforce book—without putting in so much that it would betray that my affection for her had temporarily eclipsed that of my affection for Wilberforce himself (my affection for them is now equal, but different)—and I desperately hoped that someone would write a full popular biography of her as soon as possible.

I'm thrilled to say my friend Karen Swallow Prior has done just that, and I vigorously commend to the reader her excellent and entertaining book *Fierce Convictions: The Extraordinary Life of Hannah More—Poet, Reformer, Abolitionist* from which I gather much of the information in this chapter. But until you have that estimable volume in your hands, I offer this sketch.

◆ ◆ ◆

Hannah More was born in the reign of King George II, on February 2, 1745, the fourth of five daughters born to Jacob and Mary More in a small four-room cottage in Stapleton in Gloucestershire. Jacob More was the schoolmaster at a charity school at Fishponds, the village where they lived. But Jacob and Mary educated their four girls at home, giving them an education far superior to what most girls received at that time. Indeed girls in those days did not get much by way of education at all.

All the girls were bright, but from the earliest age Hannah was recognized as especially so. At age three she widened the eyes of the local vicar by reciting her catechism at church and took home a sixpence for the performance. By four she could read and write, and her love for writing grew apace. Every year as her birthday approached, Hannah requested paper, something scarce and expensive at that time. She was endlessly writing poems and essays.

From the earliest age, she was known for her sharp tongue and quick wit as well as for a remarkable memory. But she was also known for having a distinctly moral bent, often imbuing her writings with particular lessons, a penchant that would follow her throughout her life. Hannah was also a somewhat sickly child, and the family used it as an excuse to dote on her.

Jacob and Mary hoped their five daughters would open a school of their own someday, and Jacob More steered their home education in that direction. In 1758 Hannah's eldest sister, Mary, then twenty, fulfilled her parents' expectations and opened a girls boarding school in Bristol. Hannah was thirteen and enrolled as a student, but at age sixteen she joined her older sisters—Mary, Betty, and Sally—in teaching at the school.

The school was aimed at the growing middle class in the economically thriving city. Following in their father's advanced footsteps, Hannah and her sisters thought women's education should not be significantly different from that offered to men. Throughout her life Hannah was an outspoken advocate of educational reforms for women. She was also a believer in engaging the imagination in education, something that was considered unorthodox at that time. Years later she wrote that teachers should avoid "mere verbal rituals and dry systems."[3] She considered it crucial to communicate lessons as lively and invitingly as possible.

Living in the cultural and social swirl of Bristol must have been exhilarating to a young woman of Hannah's talents and affinities. The city's prosperous economy drew the noble, smart, and fashionable, and the events and opportunities on offer stood in starkest comparison to life at Fishponds. When she was sixteen the charming and vivacious Hannah befriended the renowned Scottish astronomer, globe maker, and portraitist James Ferguson, who was in town delivering lectures on experimental philosophy. Two years later, in 1763, she attended a lecture by Thomas Sheridan, who was the godson of Jonathan Swift and the father of the great poet and playwright Richard Sheridan. Hannah struck up a friendship with Sheridan after he read one of her poems, and he encouraged her in her writing. Her talent at winning the trust and friendship of notable people followed her through life.

That same year, the eighteen-year-old Hannah wrote her first play, titled *The Search After Happiness*, a pastoral drama in verse, intended to be performed by the girls at the school. Like much of what she would write the years ahead, it was greatly entertaining, but it also had a moral sensibility, something sorely lacking in similar plays of the time. It was this lack that prompted her to write the play in the first place, as the often off-color content of what was available was certainly not appropriate for the girls Hannah was teaching.

The Theatre Royal opened in Bristol to great fanfare a few years later in 1766. Many of the school's students had ties to the theater, and frequent student outings to dramatic performances became a regular part of the school's offering. This held great appeal for parents wishing to expose their daughters to culture. Hannah became close friends with theater manager William Powell, toast of the London stage.

In 1767 Hannah visited the nearby estate of William Turner, who was cousin to two students at the Mores' school. Turner was in every way a gentleman, possessing excellent character, education, breeding, and taste. He was wealthy too. His estate, called Belmont, was only a few miles from Bristol, so when his two younger cousins came to spend their holidays, Hannah and her younger sister, Patty, accompanied them. Though Hannah was two decades his junior, she always seemed beyond her years, and the two shared many overlapping affinities. Within the year he proposed marriage, and Hannah gladly accepted.

The new and glamorous life that now lay ahead would be dramatically different from what she had known as a teacher or as a child growing up in her parents' humble cottage. She immediately began preparations for her future as the Lady of Belmont: she gave up her share in her sisters' school and began spending much time and money buying clothes suited to the life she would soon be leading. But not that soon. The engagement lasted six years, during which time Hannah visited Turner often and appropriately played the role of wife-to-be, consulting with her future husband on everything, including the landscaping and design of the gardens that adorned Belmont's impressive grounds. Turner had some of More's poems engraved and posted on plaques around the estate and even gave her a cottage to use as a place to write, naming it after her.

In time, quite as expected, a date was set for their wedding, and preparations made. But suddenly Turner had a change of mind. He did not wish to end their engagement, only to postpone it. So another date was set, but Turner suffered cold feet again. A third date was set, and—in typical fashion—Turner postponed it once more. But for the very patient Hannah, this was the end. Though Turner earnestly begged her to forgive him and not to end the engagement, saying she could pick the wedding date herself and he would promise to stick to it, Hannah was adamant that it must now be broken once and for all. Her sisters strongly encouraged her in this decision.

As was common in those days, Turner arranged to provide Hannah with the considerable annual sum of two hundred pounds in recompense. She staunchly refused, but her sisters would not have it. They forced her to change her mind and accept. It would be this money that enabled her to do much of her writing in the years to come.

In the meantime, however, the discord was more than Hannah could bear, and she suffered some sort of nervous breakdown. While recovering in Weston-super-Mare, about twenty miles from Bristol, she met and befriended Dr. James Langhorne, the vicar of Blagdon. He was a translator and, like herself, a poet. Their friendship soon blossomed, and Langhorne—who had lost two wives in childbirth—proposed marriage. But Hannah refused. Why she did so we can never know, but she remained good friends with Langhorne for the rest of her life. Twenty years later, she even resumed her friendship with William Turner, who never overcame letting her slip away.

But it was now, after Hannah had rejected the idea of marriage, that the world of London opened to her, and with London, all else besides.

◆ ◆ ◆

H annah visited the great city for the first time in 1774, at the age of twenty-nine. She took in the famous historical and literary sites and befriended David Garrick, then the best-known actor in London and manager of London's Theatre Royal. James Stonhouse, a longtime family friend who wished to support Hannah in her literary ambitions, had forwarded a manuscript of her play, *The Inflexible Captive*, to Garrick. The play had already been staged in Bristol to rave reviews. But it was not until her second trip to the city that the opportunity arose to meet Garrick. When they met at his home in London's Westminster section, the actor and his wife hit it off with Hannah immediately. That one meeting commenced the strongest friendship of all their lives.

Garrick flung open the bronze doors of the city's sanctum sanctorum and introduced his new friend to a veritable who's who of late eighteenth-century London. She was soon enjoying the company of the great cultural figures of that day, including the playwright Richard Sheridan; the conservative parliamentarian Edmund Burke; the famous portraitist Sir Joshua Reynolds; and the celebrated Edward Gibbon, author of the epic *History of the Decline and Fall of the Roman Empire*, and whose work Hannah once characterized as "fine, but insidious." [4] If this weren't enough, she soon became friends with none other than the renowned and everywhere-celebrated Dr. Samuel Johnson.

Hannah's introduction to the man, who two decades before had created the first dictionary in the English language, could not have been better scripted. Joshua Reynolds warned her of Johnson's foul moods, but Johnson entered with a dazzling parrot perched on his hand and a line from Hannah's poetry on his lips. Their friendship was off to a roaring start and never flagged. They entertained each other and were so fond of each other that, though they were separated by thirty-five years, people often teased them about their affections for one another.

In a letter to one of her sisters, Hannah wrote, "I had the happiness to [walk] Dr. Johnson home from Hill Street, though Mrs. Montagu publicly declared she did not think it prudent to trust us together, with such a declared affection on both sides. She said she was afraid of a Scotch elopement."[5] The law requiring an announcement three weeks before a wedding did not apply in Scotland. Montague, convener of the exclusive literary and intellectual circle to which Hannah was a frequent guest, was worried the pair might get carried away and slip up north.

Because of her humble beginnings, Hannah often felt she must be dreaming to find herself in this vaunted cultural and social Elysium. At times she wore a social insecurity about her, and those who disliked her or who, like Johnson's celebrated biographer James Boswell, were jealous of her, often took base swipes at her in print. But all who knew her for the wit and charm would never believe she thought herself unworthy of their company. Johnson's opinion of her was perhaps the highest of all. He called her "the most powerful versificatrix" in the English language.[6] When someone mentioned poetry at a gathering, Johnson interrupted: "Hush, hush. It is dangerous to say a word of poetry before her. It is talking of the art of war before Hannibal."[7]

In the *Nine Living Muses*, Richard Samuel's painting that today hangs in London's National Gallery, Hannah is pictured as Melpomene, the Muse of Tragedy. But Garrick and his wife sometimes called their friend by the pet nickname "Nine," meaning they thought her to be the very embodiment of all the muses combined.

Hannah quickly grew so close to the Garricks that she became their semi-permanent house guest. Garrick's wife, Eva Marie, was a celebrated beauty who had danced in the courts of Europe, and the childless couple adopted the charming spinster as an intimate member of their small family. Hannah returned to London for six or more weeks each year and lived with them. Hannah was David Garrick's greatest fan and boasted of once seeing him on stage twenty-seven times in a season. But he admired her writing every bit as much as she admired his acting, and he once made the present to her of an inkstand carved from the wood of a mulberry tree that belonged to Shakespeare.

In 1774 Hannah's play, *The Inflexible Captive*, was published by Thomas Caddell. A year later he published two more volumes, *Sir Eldred and the Bower* and *The Ballad of Bleeding Rock*. Hannah's pen never stopped nor seemed even to slow for very long. Caddell cashed in and became her publisher for the next forty years.[8]

In 1777 the Covent Garden Theater produced Hannah's play *Percy*, a tragedy. This was a tremendous honor, but perhaps greater yet was that Garrick wrote both the play's prologue and epilogue. She attended the premier with the Garricks and was overwhelmed at the "bursts of applause" it drew.[9] It proved to be a smash success. Indeed, it was literally the most acclaimed play of that era. The printers blew through four thousand copies in the span of two weeks. Productions were mounted across England and then in France and Austria too.

Hannah's Christian faith and moral bent were less pronounced now than they would eventually become, but they were nonetheless an important part of how she saw the world and what she wrote. Garrick was by no means a serious Christian, but he was greatly respectful of Hannah's faith. It is in her ready acceptance and love of those who did not share her faith that we see an important aspect of Hannah More. She did not let the indifference or even the irreligiosity of most in these circles dissuade her from enjoying their company. Like her future friend Wilberforce, she did not lose her wit when she found God.

The success of *Percy* led Garrick to urge Hannah to write another play, which she did. It was titled *The Fatal Falsehood*, and its principal theme was self-restraint, or "self-conquest," to use Hannah's phrase:

[I]f to govern realms belong to few,
Yet all who live have passions to subdue.
Self-conquest is the lesson books should preach,
Self-conquest is the theme the stages should teach.[10]

Garrick himself helped guide Hannah in her writing of the play, but in January 1779, a month before his sixty-second birthday, he died. He was so beloved by the nation that he was accorded the honor of being the first actor to be buried in the Poets' Corner at Westminster Abbey. "I am disappointed by that stroke of death," Johnson wrote, "which has eclipsed the gaiety of nations, and impoverished the public stock of harmless pleasure."[11] Hannah continued to live with Garrick's widow, Eva Marie, who was her dearest friend, but their grief at his loss was considerable.

A few months later Hannah took the play she had written to Covent Garden. It was produced almost immediately, but Hannah was too sick to attend when the curtain on it rose in May. It's just as well that she was absent. During the second night of the performance, Hannah Cowley, a dramatist and poet in attendance, shot up in her seat. "That's mine!" she yelled. "That's mine!" Garrick had mentored Cowley as well. Was there some overlap in his direction? Hannah was mortified and denied any wrongdoing. Indeed, the supposed plagiarism would prove unfounded, but Hannah was so bruised by the incident that she decided the play was no longer the thing and thenceforth abandoned writing for the stage.

◆ ◆ ◆

That an unmarried woman via her own talents and efforts could rise from humble circumstances to eventual fame and great wealth was an idea far ahead of its time. Social mobility of any kind was not the norm in the late eighteenth and early nineteenth centuries, so a poor schoolmaster's daughter mixing with London's elites was remarkable. Perhaps more remarkable yet is her acceptance as an equal by many of the most prominent men of her era.

Hannah's idea that a large part of women's education should be to make them better companions in marriage may seem backward today, but it was forward-thinking for the time. "Indeed," says Karen Swallow Prior, "the companionate marriage—rather than the politically or economically expedient one that had been the norm for all of human history—was an idea advanced by evangelicals, including Hannah, who understood marriage to be an institution established to advance the kingdom of God, not property."[12] Hannah was no feminist, but her Christian understanding of the spiritual equality between men and women was far ahead of its time and did much to advance women toward a greater role in public life. She participated in some social circles that had been the exclusive precinct of men. In fact, one weekly men's meeting—calling itself the "Sour-crout Party" from its regular menu—always opened its doors to her.

But with the death of Garrick and the misfortune over *The Fatal Falsehood*, Hannah began a slow withdrawal from London and the exciting life she had lived over the previous five years. They were now days of transition. The social swirl that had once been so appealing became less so, and the Christian faith that had always been a part of the background of her life began to move into the foreground. Prior writes: "More became increasingly disenchanted with the trappings of high society and turned more fully toward the Christian faith she had assumed all her life but not embraced with full intention."[13]

The principal catalyst for this was John Newton's book *Cardiphonia*, which More read in 1780. Newton was the former slave ship captain who embraced Christian faith and gave up the trade, eventually becoming a minister in the Church of England and writing the famous hymn, "Amazing Grace." Embracing much of the new evangelical message of George Whitefield and John Wesley, Newton was no run-of-the-mill Anglican. In a letter to one of her sisters about *Cardiphonia*, Hannah wrote, "There is in it much vital religion, and much of the experience of a good Christian, who feels and laments his own imperfections and weaknesses."[14] Hannah recommended the book to everyone she knew. "I like it prodigiously," she said.[15]

That same year she befriended that "sacriligeous charmer," Horace Walpole. Walpole was a celebrated cynic and rake who had an early homosexual affair with the poet Thomas Gray, invented the Gothic novel, wrote a definitive, though extremely catty memoir of the Georgian period, and coined the word *serendipity*.

Hannah and Walpole would remain lifelong friends, but the dissonance between what she believed and what he and most of her other friends in London society believed had begun to concern her. Writing to Newton, she said, "I know that many people whom I hear say a thousand brilliant and agreeable things disbelieve, or at least disregard, those truths on which I found my everlasting hopes."[16] She felt herself being pulled between two worlds. Much like Wilberforce, who thought getting serious about God might mean leaving the world behind, including politics, so Hannah More thought she might need to leave London and its elite cultural circles, along with status as their much-sought-after darling. Hannah would indeed leave London, but it was her ability to be friends with these people with whom she disagreed that set her apart from many Methodists and pietists and that would make her singularly effective as an agent of cultural change.

In the meantime, however, she was still working these things out and feeling uncomfortable. To turn her back on the theater was no small thing, but she now could not help feeling the pointlessness of much of what passed for life in London society. For example, women's obsession with fashion—which at that time expressed itself in increasingly outrageous hats—suddenly seemed too much to bother with. But neither did she wish to openly buck the fashion trends, lest in being unfashionable it appear she were trying to draw attention to herself! It was a conundrum.

Hannah's growing objections to the stage did not extend to her views on literature in general. Indeed, her writings during the period following Garrick's death "saw no inconsistency between the devoutest piety and the cultivation of elegant literature and taste," as her biographer Henry Thompson put it.[17] Hannah knew the power of dramatic literature and was drawn to employing that influence toward didactic ends. In 1782 she publicly signaled her growing faith when she published *Sacred Dramas*, dramatizations of various Bible stories in verse. Hannah More understood that the culture in which one lived was as much or more influenced by the arts than by legislation, and she undertook to use her gifts in God's service. She did not wish to retreat from culture into a religious sphere, but rather to advance with the wisdom and truth of religion into the cultural sphere.

But as it is today with Christians trying to accomplish similar things, atheists and secularists were not her only trouble. Pietistic Christians took umbrage at the idea of mixing the things of the Bible and God with the things of the world. Hannah saw the folly in such thinking and stood firmly against it. "I hope the poets and painters will at last bring the Bible into fashion," she wrote, "and that people will get to like it from taste, though they are insensible to its spirits, and afraid of its doctrines."[18] She was a pioneer and, like all pioneers, took grief from those she was leaving behind and those she encountered as she blazed her new trails. As Prior puts it, "Neither the literary elite nor the strict religionists were pleased."[19]

Even her friend Samuel Johnson took the "religious" line of that day and spoke against dramatizing or touching the stories in the Bible. "All amplification is frivolous and vain," he said. "All addition to that which is already sufficient for the purpose of religion, seems not only useless, but in some degree profane." He felt that the events of the Bible, inasmuch as God himself scripted them, were "above the power of human genius to dignify."[20] When a decade later it was announced that someone planned to produce a stage production of one of the stories from *Sacred Dramas*, it was not angry atheists who were up in arms, but the town's religious conservatives.

Though she adored Johnson, Hannah would disagree with him on something else during this period. He had famously quipped that to be tired of London was to be tired of life. Hannah was not tired of life, but she had surely grown tired of London. In a way it was Johnson's own death that confirmed her desire to leave the fabled city for new pastures. For Hannah, David Garrick and Samuel Johnson were the very best of London, and after the latter's death in 1784, both of them were gone and, with them, most of what tied her to life in the city. So in 1785 Hannah set up house at Cowslip Green, a cottage in Somerset's Mendip Hills. There she could spend her hours gardening.

It was a dramatic change from big-city life, but an even greater change was underway by 1787. That was the year she met both John Newton and William Wilberforce and joined them in the great battle for the abolition of the slave trade.

◆ ◆ ◆

Newton had as storied a life as one can imagine. He was an exceedingly rough man who became a slave ship captain, but who in the midst of a life-threatening storm at sea surrendered his life to God. He eventually left the slave trade and became a minister in the Church of England, though he avoided the skim milk of French Enlightenment rationalism preached from most Church of England pulpits and ardently embraced a "vital Christianity" as Methodist as it was Anglican.

While in his forties he often did what was called "parlour preaching" in the homes of wealthy people, and at the home of John Thornton he met the nine-year-old William Wilberforce. During the next two years Newton became something of a father figure to the boy. But Wilberforce's mother was horrified when she caught wind of his being exposed to Methodism and dragged him back to Hull, where he was forbidden even from attending church, lest he have his incipient faith rekindled. In time, Wilberforce lost what faith he had, but at age twenty-six, on a journey to the French and Italian Rivieras, he found it again.

That year, 1785, he visited his old friend John Newton—then sixty—and Newton encouraged him to stay in politics, so that God could use him there. But how would God use him? "God almighty has set before me two great objects," Wilberforce wrote in his diary two years later, "the suppression of the slave trade and the reformation of manners." This was the great calling to which Wilberforce would devote himself for the rest of his life. And it was none other than Hannah More who would be his closest collaborator in both of these "great objects."

Though Hannah had maintained a correspondence with Newton, she had never met him in person. But in 1787 she made a pilgrimage to his church, St. Mary Woolnoth in London. She attended service and afterward spent an hour speaking with this great man who had already so influenced her. It was principally her friendship with Newton that turned Hannah toward a more evangelical faith.

That same year she met William Wilberforce in Bath. "That young man's character is one of the most extraordinary I have ever known for talent, virtue, and piety," she told her sisters. "It is difficult not to grow better and wiser every time one converses with him."[21] Their relationship was immediate and magnetic, and it was one of the most enduring and significant of her life. How Wilberforce came to be the chief champion of abolition—and how he was able to succeed in ending the slave trade in Great Britain in 1807, after twenty years of battling—has everything to do with Hannah More.

The story began nine years earlier, in 1776, when Hannah met Sir Charles and Margaret Middleton, who had an estate in Teston. Their clergyman was a certain James Ramsay, who had seen the unspeakable horrors of the slave trade firsthand and who succeeded in influencing the Middletons that something must be done. Lady Middleton became especially passionate about the topic and had many dinner parties at which the issue was discussed. Thus was Hannah drawn into the fray. But they eventually realized that abolition must have a champion in Parliament, and they soon settled on Wilberforce, inviting him to consider it. After some prayer and reflection, Wilberforce accepted the role: he would lead the charge against the slave trade in Parliament. But just as Hannah and her friends needed someone in politics to help them, so Wilberforce desperately needed someone in the world of culture to help him, and Hannah was that person.

So when in 1788 Wilberforce decided it was time to bring to Parliament his bill abolishing the slave trade, Hannah began work on "Slavery," a poem designed to help sway public opinion on the slave trade, and specifically to influence the voting on Wilberforce's bill. "I am now busily engaged on a poem, to be called 'Slavery,'" she wrote her sister: "I grieve I did not set about it sooner; as it must now be done in such a hurry as no poem should ever be written in, to be properly correct; but, good or bad, if it does not come out at the particular moment when the discussion comes on in parliament, it will not be worth a straw."[22]

For all her protestations, it was an excellent poem. No less than the poet William Cowper thought it so admirable that he scotched his own plans to compose one along similar lines.

The genius of the abolitionists—and the likely reason for their ultimate success—is that they understood that their battle was not merely political and went to great lengths to make the cultural case against slavery and the trade as well. Josiah Wedgwood created a famous image of a slave in chains with the motto "Am I Not a Man and a Brother?" that was reproduced everywhere, and a poster was created that showed how tightly packed the slaves were on the slave ships. These and other things touched people's hearts and contributed to turning the popular tide against slavery. But it was Hannah's pen that did the most.

Her role in the war against slavery can hardly be overstated. She helped the average Briton see the humanity of the African slaves for the first time—as mothers, fathers, and children little different from their white, British counterparts. Most of Hannah's readers had never even seen an African and thought of slavery as an abstract economic necessity. But with her great poetic powers, Hannah helped them see that the slave trade caused tremendous suffering, that to support slavery meant supporting a practice that tore infants from the breasts of their mothers. Her words pricked the consciences of millions, who came to feel that their country—which called itself a Christian country—must have no part in such an evil. Eventually hundreds of thousands of Britons signed petitions against the slave trade, which were brought by Wilberforce into Parliament and swayed its members toward abolition.

Another important figure who was friends with Hannah More was Beilby Porteus, whose role in abolition and other social reforms is rarely fully appreciated. Porteus was an evangelical who in 1787 was made bishop of London. "I rejoice for many reasons," Hannah wrote on hearing the news, "but for none more than that his ecclesiastical jurisdiction, extending to the West Indies, will make him of infinite usefulness in the great object I have so much at heart—the project to abolish the slave-trade in Africa."[23] Porteus would indeed do all he could to help Hannah and her friends in their battles for abolition and the other social evils of that day, and he could do a lot. He was also the one Hannah credited as having influenced her toward using her literary gifts for God's purposes—specifically for Wilberforce's two "great objects." And what of the second?

◆ ◆ ◆

I n 1788, in addition to writing "Slavery," Hannah undertook a second major writing project. She knew that many of the social evils of that day—especially the slave trade—stemmed from the worldview of most Britons, who thought of themselves as Christians, but who were in reality and in practice pagans and agnostics. They might have attended church, but it was a mere formality, and their lives did not exhibit anything like the robust—the word in those days was "vital"— faith that Hannah had experienced and knew possible for all. So she now wrote a book titled *Thoughts on the Importance of the Manners of the Great to General Society.*

Hannah More and Wilberforce both knew that it was the elites who set the fashion not just in clothing, but in people's behavior too. And in general the immorality and irreligiosity of the upper classes at that time can hardly be believed. For example, the Prince of Wales, who would become King George IV, was a notorious ne'er-do-well who racked up astronomical gambling debts—which were paid by the taxpayers from the national treasury—and who was rumored to have bedded thousands of women over the serpentine course of his dissolute life. The effect of these practices on the middle and lower classes was powerful, so Wilberforce determined that they, as John Pollock memorably put it, would "make goodness fashionable."[24] Legislation was not enough, so he and Hannah worked hard to influence the cultural elites directly. But events of the next year would make this job even harder than it would otherwise be.

The French Revolution erupted in 1789, causing major changes in the political and cultural climate in England. The radical ideas that were causing the streets to run with blood in Paris were alive in London, too, and that the violence and revolution did not leap across the Channel and rout the British way of life is in large part once again due to the pen of Hannah More.

Hannah was persuaded by friends that she must use her gifts to counter the destructive ideas being put forward by Thomas Paine in the cheap pamphlets that were so popular in those days. In a letter to the Earl of Oxford, Hannah wrote, "I happened to know of a good many of the religious people, both in the church and among the different sects, whose fondness for French politics entirely blinds them to the horrors of French impiety."[25] So she wrote a pamphlet much like the ones that Paine was producing, but which exposed the deep anti-clericalism that lay behind most of the French radicalism. She titled it *Village Politics* and published it under the pseudonym "Will Chip." To divert suspicions of her authorship, she sent the manuscript to a different publisher than Caddell—the ruse worked for a while.

There had never been anything like it, and the hunger for *Village Politics* was stunning. She addressed the pamphlet to "The Mechanics, Journeymen, and Labourers, in Great Britain," but it seemed as if everyone wanted a copy.[26] Hundreds of thousands circulated in London and beyond, including Scotland and Ireland. Patriotic citizens printed reams at their own expense. But the wild success meant the author could not hide behind her *nom de plume* for long. Eventually Hannah's identity was out in the open, and she was soon credited by many with preventing revolution on English soil.

In August of that same year, Wilberforce and his sister paid a visit to Hannah and her sisters at Cowslip Green. While there, he decided to take an excursion. Nearby Cheddar Gorge was known for its beauty, but Wilberforce was caught off guard by the poverty of the villagers there. When he returned to Cowslip Green, he was clearly upset, so much so that he skipped the evening meal to be alone in his room. When he later emerged, the sensitive and generous Wilberforce told Hannah More and her sister Patty what he had seen and what he proposed as a solution. He said that if they "would be at the trouble" to help those poor people, he would "be at the expense."[27]

This launched one of the greatest successes of Hannah More's life, the so-called Sunday schools of that region, which were not church schools for religious instruction, as Sunday schools are today, but actual schools that were open on Sunday, when workers had the day off. The idea behind these schools was, as she explained, "to train up the lower classes to habits of industry and piety."[28]

Hannah's initial and ongoing efforts to educate the poor of the Cheddar region of Somerset were simply heroic, even Herculean. But she knew what was at stake. Education, specifically in religion, would go a long way toward lifting these people out of the morass of hopelessness and criminality so rampant among them. At first, she worked hard simply to persuade the poor to send their children to these schools, but it was often the wealthy and influential people of a region who were most opposed to her. Part of this has to do with the fact that education is an equalizing force, one thought by many to be destabilizing and therefore to be discouraged at all costs. But many of the wealthy also thought religion itself was the problem.

One of Hannah's letters to Wilberforce provides a startling example. "I was told we should meet with great opposition if I did not try to propitiate the chief despot of the village, who is very rich and very brutal, so I ventured to the den of this monster," she wrote. The man informed her that religion was "the worst thing in the world for the poor, for it made them lazy and useless."[29] She did all she could to persuade the man, but failed nonetheless. As a result, Hannah became discouraged. Was enlisting the wealthy even worth the trouble? She knew the schools could never succeed without the local gentry on her side—or at least not fighting her. So she continued, making eleven more visits to unpleasant and disagreeable souls in their large houses. She wrote to Wilberforce of her efforts:

> Miss Wilberforce would have been shocked, had she seen the petty tyrants whose insolence I stroked and tamed, the ugly children I praised, the pointers and spaniels I caressed, the cider I commended, and the wine I swallowed. . . . [T]hey are as ignorant as the beasts that perish, intoxicated every day before dinner, and plunged in such vices as make me begin to think London a virtuous place.[30]

The poverty, ignorance, and immorality of many in these villages was truly shocking, but Hannah and Patty More waded in fearlessly, even though they were often warned not to venture into these wretched areas for the sake of their own safety. The Church of England had abandoned most of these villages, leaving their inhabitants to live under the

despotism of the chief landowners and farmers and in complete ignorance of the Christian faith.

In a letter to John Newton, Hannah wrote, "One great benefit which
I have found to result from our projects, is the removal of that great
gulf which has divided the rich and poor in these country parishes, by
making them meet together; whereas before, they hardly thought they
were children of one common [F]ather."[31] But it was this very whiff
of egalitarianism that caused many to oppose her work, assuming it
would lead to the kind of rebellion as was raging across France.

Still, the effort was a glorious success. Before long there were
three hundred children attending the school in Cheddar, and within a
decade, Hannah and Patty had set up twelve schools in the neighbor-
ing villages. They built on these successes by adding evening classes
for adults and weekday classes for girls. By the 1850s, 75 percent of
all laboring-class children between five and fifteen were enrolled in
Sunday schools.

◆ ◆ ◆

Perhaps one of the reasons Hannah More is regarded as the most
influential woman of her time is that she had the singular ability to use her writing skills to influence both the educated wealthy as
well as the uneducated poor. She and Wilberforce knew that this two-
pronged approach was necessary to bring about change in the culture
of that time.

In 1791 Hannah once more focused her writing on those in the upper
classes. She published a book that was essentially a sequel to *Thoughts
on the Importance of the Manners of the Great to General Society*. It
was titled *An Estimate of the Religion of the Fashionable World*. In the
book, she wanted to speak about those of the "more decent class" who
"acknowledge their belief of its truth by a public profession, and are not
inattentive to any of its forms, yet exhibit little of its spirit in their general temper and conduct."[32] She went so far as to compare these people

to Christ's betrayer, Judas, right in the introduction. She made the case, and it struck a chord. Because of her deft genius as a writer, and because of the great esteem in which she was held as a result, Hannah could say strong things in a way that was generally accepted, even by those on the receiving end of such strong words.

But in 1795 she would turn her writing skills back toward the poorer and less educated. The wild success of *Village Politics* encouraged Hannah to continue writing similar tracts, which in 1795 she began to produce at the prodigious rate of three per month. The antireligious tracts of Thomas Paine continued to be all the rage. Roberts writes that they worked "to undermine, not only religious establishments, but good government, by the alluring vehicles of novels, stories, and songs."[33] So Hannah felt she must fight them on their own turf. In writing these tracts, she was fighting fire with fire. These destructive ideas needed to be countered, and she wrote the tracts intentionally to compete with what was already popular.

But as with so much that Hannah did, it was the entire network of what would come to be known as the Clapham Sect that made success possible. Her wealthy friend Henry Thornton enabled these tracts to be sold for significantly less than what the other tracts sold for, and this strategy worked. Before a year had passed, two million copies sold. These Cheap Repository Tracts, as they were known, were published from March 1795 through September 1798. Hannah wrote half of the approximately one hundred and oversaw the writing of the rest. A number of them aimed specifically to awaken the middle and lower classes to the humanity of the Africans their own country was enslaving and working to death in the West Indies.

Of course it was one thing to talk of the humanity of these Africans and another to actually treat them as equals. But in 1797 when the abolitionists got involved in the issue of Sierra Leone, a West African colony established by the British Crown for freed Africans, they sent a number of African children to England, to be educated at Hannah More's schools. A number of these children also spent time at

Clapham, playing with Wilberforce's children and the children of the other abolitionists who lived there.

Trying to explain what "the Clapham Sect" was is not easy, especially inasmuch as it was not a sect. Rather, it was a network of like-minded friends, most of them evangelicals, generally led by Wilberforce, who wished not only to bring an end to the slave trade but also to end the many other social evils of that era. But it was Henry Thornton who in 1795 decided to create an environment that would foster these efforts. He realized that if many of these friends lived near each other, it would facilitate what they were trying to accomplish. They could gather in each other's homes and discuss and plan and encourage one another.

So he began expanding his own large house in Clapham, which would eventually boast thirty-six bedrooms, and he also built two more large houses adjacent. He persuaded his dear friend Wilberforce to move there with his wife and six children, and very quickly a number of their other friends followed suit. They all attended the church in Clapham, Holy Trinity, where their friend John Venn preached. Granville Sharp, Isaac Milner, Charles Simeon, Zachary Macauley, and many other notable figures of that time were a vital part of it, but none was more vital than Hannah More.

Like Wilberforce, she seemed to be involved in a hundred things at once. She was forever working to expand the reach of her Sunday schools. In 1796, she wrote of a "new parish, so surprisingly wicked and inconceivably ignorant that I feel when there as if I were queen of Botany Bay," a reference to an infamous Australian penal colony.[34] Also like Wilberforce, she continued to be attacked, not just from those on the atheistic left, who thought her a moralistic busy-body, but from those on the traditional right, who thought her efforts were undermining their way of life. "I hear with little emotion," she wrote, "such attacks on the supposed violence of my aristocratic principles; you know how much more I have had to sustain from my supposed attachment to democrats and dissenters."[35]

In 1799, seeing the vital role women were beginning to play in culture, and one that she encouraged, Hannah wrote and published *Strictures on the Modern System of Female Education*. The book sets forth a high, biblical view of women, on the one side fighting off Rousseau's misogynistic doctrine of "sensibility," which regards women as "frivolous creatures of mere emotion and sentiment," and on the other fighting off the proto-feminist Mary Wollstonecraft's notion of women's "rights.". In 1792 Wollstonecraft published her now famous book, *Vindication of the Rights of Woman*, but Hannah was in no wise enamored of the views it set out. "[T]here is something fantastic and absurd in the very title," she wrote. "How many ways there are of being ridiculous! I am sure I have as much liberty as I can make a good use of, now I am an old maid; and when I was a young one, I had, I dare say, more than was good for me."[36]

The year 1799 also marked the beginning of another painful episode for Hannah because of something that came to be known as the "the Blagdon Controversy." Blagdon was a town where in 1795 Hannah had established one of her Sunday schools. In a letter to Wilberforce from that time, she told of the early successes they were having in this particularly difficult place:

Several of the grown-up youths had been tried at the last assizes [periodic criminal courts]; three were children of a person lately condemned to be hanged—many thieves! [A]ll ignorant, profane, and vicious beyond belief! Of this banditti we have enlisted one hundred and seventy; and when the clergyman, a hard man, who is also the magistrate, saw these creatures kneeling around us, whom he had seldom seen but to commit or punish in some way, he burst into tears.[37]

But it was this same minister who would four years later start all the trouble, violently objecting to the supposed "Methodism" in one of the schoolteachers.

The genius of Hannah was that she was able to teach "vital Christianity"—which one typically saw only in Methodist circles—but to keep everything officially under the auspices of the Church of England by working only with Anglican churches and teaming up with Church of England ministers. She knew that the desiccated tradition of the Church of England had failed all these poor people, and she knew that the evangelical Methodism of Wesley and Whitefield was what they needed to revive their interest in God—and it was what caused so many of them to change their lives for the better.

But she also knew that she must be wary of seeming to be "officially" Methodist, lest those in the Church of England think her and her schools were being merely subversive of the established order. Because of what was happening in France, anything that was not traditionally English or that meant to lift up the poor was in danger of being thought radical and "revolutionary." It was an extremely polarized time, when the slightest feint in the direction of liberty or egalitarianism was seen as a leap toward the bloody chaos across the Channel.

Because of Hannah's fame, what began as a local affair was soon fanned into a conflagration by the London papers. The "Blagdon Controversy"—in which she was over and over accused of Methodism and therefore of undermining traditional values—raged on for nearly three years and took a great toll on her, eventually causing her to have what seemed another nervous breakdown.

◆ ◆ ◆

n 1801 Hannah thought it was time to move from her cottage at Cowslip Green to something larger. So she began building Barley Wood, the capacious estate where she lived for most of the next three decades.

As ever, the writing continued, most of it in a moralistic vein, before "moralistic" had become a pejorative. In 1805 she published *Hints Towards Forming the Character of a Young Princess,* which sets forth the idea of a monarch as a moral leader, and in 1808, she anonymously published her only novel, *Coelebs in Search of a Wife*. The two questions that obsessed London society when it came out were "Who was the author?" and "How should one pronounce 'Coelebs'?" As with so much else she wrote, this two-volume novel was an immediate best seller. In its pages she again put forward the progressive idea of a "companionate marriage," based not on economic advancement or political prudence, as were most marriages in those days, but on personal compatibility. Here again, we have the powerful advocacy of the prescient Hannah to thank for pushing forward something we now take entirely for granted.

In 1813 Hannah and her friends in the Clapham Circle would take on another vitally important initiative. It concerned a bill to send Anglican missionaries to India. Wilberforce reckoned it second in importance only to his crusade against the slave trade. He had tried and failed to pass a similar bill in 1793, when the East India Company's charter came up for renewal. Now, two decades later, when it came up for renewal again, he was ready, and he enlisted the help of everyone in the Clapham Circle to ensure success.

Wilberforce was passionate that the East India Company and England should not merely profit from the Indian people, but should try to help them, and he knew that missionaries would introduce education, the better treatment of women, and a host of other social benefits. He was most outraged at the horrific practice of suttee, then popular, in which Indian widows were burned alive on their husband's funeral pyres. That the English were profiting handsomely from their presence in India but doing nothing to end this great evil was a moral outrage. The passage of this bill would do much toward ending the practice, but the opportunity only came around once every twenty years. It was all hands on deck. For her part, Hannah wrote an anonymous letter (signed "Philanthropos") to the *Bristol Journal*, inimitably making the case for introducing the Christian faith to India. It helped sway public opinion in this direction, and the bill passed.

But 1813 marked the beginning of a difficult time for Hannah. Her eldest sister, Mary, died. Betty would die three years later, and Sally a year later, in 1817. In 1819, Patty, the sister to whom Hannah was closest, would die. But throughout this decade and through the next, Hannah continued to write, to host a stream of visitors at Barley Wood, and to keep up a seemingly endless correspondence.

In 1821, still working to counteract the destructive irreverence of the radical literature of that time, she published *Bible Rhymes*, intended to help younger people comprehend the meaning of each of the books of the Bible. It did not sell nearly as well as her previous works, but it typified her philosophy that one must not merely rail against the darkness, but must instead light a proverbial candle by creating literary and cultural works that rival and surpass the bad.

Hannah's very last years were marked by failing health. In 1828, she moved from Barley Wood, and in 1833, at age eighty-seven, she died, just weeks after her dear friend Wilberforce. She was buried near Barley Wood, adjacent to her four sisters. But just before she died, the long effort that she and Wilberforce and their Clapham friends had worked toward finally succeeded: Parliament voted to abolish slavery throughout the British empire. One year later, innumerable African men, women, and children, whom Hannah for decades had kept before the public eye as human beings created in the image of God, would at last be freed from their chains. It is a fitting coda to her extraordinary life.

Seven years after her death, Percy Bysshe Shelley's famous essay, "In Defense of Poetry" was published. In it, as Prior points out in *Fierce Convictions*, he credited "the effects of the poetry" of Christians with ending slavery and emancipating women. The last line of his essay can serve as her fitting epitaph: "Poets are the unacknowledged legislators of the world."[38]

FOUR
Saint Maria of Paris

1891–1945

here are good reasons most people have never heard of Saint
Maria of Paris, who is also known as Maria Skobtsova. For
one thing, with every twist and turn of her life, her name itself
changed. She began life as Elizabeth Pilenko, and was called Liza.
When she married, she took her husband's name and became Elizabeth
Kuz'mina-Karavaeva. Then she divorced and married again, becoming
Elizabeth Skobtsova. She is generally referred to by that surname, but
when that marriage was annulled, she became a nun and took a new
first name: Maria. She was thenceforth known as Maria Skobtsova,
although almost everyone knew her simply as "Mother Maria." Finally,
in 2004, she was canonized by the Orthodox Church and officially
became Saint Maria of Paris.

But even if we settle on her name, her life is a welter of contra-
dictions. For example, she was born in Latvia but was ethnically
Ukrainian. She lived her early years in Russia and then moved back

to the Ukraine. Then after the Russian Revolution she moved to Paris, where she lived until she was taken to Ravensbrück, in Germany.

What she did can also be confusing. First, she was a poet who swam among the literary elites of St. Petersburg; then she managed her family's award-winning wine estate on the Black Sea—and became the mayor of the town there. When the Russian Revolution made life impossible, she moved to Paris and became a nun. Finally, even as a nun she confounds our expectations: she smoked and drank. She did not live in a monastery but considered the whole world her monastery. She married twice, divorced twice, and had three children by two different men. Yet for all of this woman's dramatically unorthodox behavior, the Orthodox Church recognizes her as a saint. Can we be blamed for being confused about this extraordinary woman?

In truth, it is precisely because of all these things that she commands our attention. Her life was messy and complicated, as most of ours are messy and complicated. By breaking every mold in which we would put her, she shows forth the beauty and the full-throated reality of the Christian life in a way that few in history have ever done.

One reason I find her compelling is because of the striking similarities between her life and that of Dietrich Bonhoeffer. Both were brilliant and grew up in an elite, intellectual atmosphere. Both eschewed "religiosity" or "pietism," and both smoked and drank. Both were profoundly enamored of the idea that Jesus was fully incarnate; and that in his humanity he connected us to God in a way that is so direct as to be shocking and life-changing—if we can only grasp it. Both wrote brilliantly and knew that their writings meant nothing if they did not live them out. Both were less interested in meeting the expectations of their own church denomination than in helping their denomination meet the expectations of God himself. Both understood it was the duty of every Christian to stand up for the Jews being persecuted by the Nazis; and both, because they did this, were murdered in concentration camps just weeks before the war ended. The parallels really are astonishing.

Finally, I wished to include this great woman because many of us know of Christian heroes from the Protestant and Catholic traditions, but few of us know of the heroes of the Orthodox tradition. I was raised in the Greek Orthodox Church, but only in later years have I come to appreciate the great treasures of Orthodoxy, and without a doubt, Maria Skobtsova—a.k.a. Mother Maria, a.k.a. Saint Maria of Paris—is one of those great treasures.

◆ ◆ ◆

lizaveta Pilenko was born in 1891 in the city of Riga in Latvia. Her family was rooted in the Ukrainian aristocracy, so her parents were well-to-do. They were also devout Orthodox Christians, and she was raised in a pious and religious atmosphere. Little Liza was passionate about serving God from her earliest years: at seven she asked her mother when she might leave home for a convent; at eight she asked permission to journey with religious pilgrims, who were visiting monasteries and shrines; and when a new church was built in her hometown, Elizabeth scraped together every bit of her savings and made a contribution to pay for the painting of a mural of her patron saint.

Liza's family moved several times, first from Riga to Anapa on the Black Sea, where her father had inherited a large estate. When she was thirteen, her father was made director of the famed Botanical Garden near Yalta, and they moved to Crimea. But the very next year—it was the summer of 1906—tragedy struck. Liza's father died. He was forty-nine, and his death hit Liza so hard that she decided she could no longer believe in God. Her beloved father's death seemed to her such an injustice that the universe appeared meaningless to her. So in the passionate way that would mark her life, she now declared herself an atheist, saying: "If there is no justice, there is no just God. Yet if there is no just God, that means there is no God at all."[1] It is unclear whether this turn was genuine or whether she was simply angry at the God in whom she now claimed not to believe.

Soon after, Liza's mother moved the family north to the city of St. Petersburg. For the first time in her life, Liza was exposed to the poor and the uneducated, and her natural compassion caused her to want to help them. The first way she helped them was by teaching them to read. But her love for these suffering people soon found another outlet in the form of Bolshevism, which had become immensely popular at that time. As a teenager, it was "the People" for whom she would fight, in deed and in word too. She began to write poems and to meet with literary people who shared her vision for a new classless future. When she was just sixteen, she met the famous poet Alexander Blok, who would have a great influence on her.

"My spirit longed to engage in heroic feats," she wrote, "even to perish, in order to combat the injustice of the world." She wished to meet others who wanted to give their all for others, who were "daily prepared to lay down their lives for the people."[2] But there was a disconnect. It seemed she mostly met people interested in *talking* about such things—and also writing poems about them and getting together to talk about the poems.

At eighteen, she impetuously married a university student who was a Bolshevik—a member of Lenin's revolutionary Social Democrats. His name was Dimitri Kuz'mina-Karavaev, so her name now became Elizabeth Kuz'mina-Karavaeva. Years later she said that she hardly knew why she married him, but the world of revolutionary ideas in which they swam was intoxicating. Her brilliance as a poet and her connections through Blok and her husband placed her in the heart of Russia's fashionable literary elite. Meetings of the newly formed Poets Guild convened in their well-appointed apartment, attracting artists and other luminaries of the intelligentsia. Elizabeth published her first book of poems during this time, titled *Scythian Shards*, a reference to the name given by the ancient Greeks to the lands bordering the northern coast of the Black Sea.

In these heady days, God and the Russian Orthodox religion held no appeal for her. She did not see the church as alive, but as a mere tradition-laden institution that was so wedded to the culture and to the Tsarist way of life that it had become ossified, had become dead and useless. But the poor people she saw everywhere engaged her mind and heart and soul. It was these people, whom she saw as rooted to the earth and the soil—to "Mother Russia"—who were real and alive, for whom she would fight. Elizabeth longed to be rooted in what was real. All the intellectual talk felt increasingly empty to her.

Meanwhile she and her husband grew apart, separating in early 1913. Immediately thereafter Elizabeth became pregnant by another man and that October gave birth to her first child. She named the girl Gaiana, which is Greek for "earthly one."

Somehow during this time, her passion for justice and for the poor would lead her back toward the Christian faith. After all, if one was seriously interested in the people of Russia, one must be interested in the faith to which most of them looked for meaning. So in that passionate, impetuous way of hers, Elizabeth now enrolled in the Ecclesiastical Academy to study theology—the first woman ever to do so.

If there was a moment when her faith returned to her full-blown, she said it was in that moment when she prayed in front of the famous 1688 icon "Mother of God, Joy of All Who Sorrow (with Coins)" in its St. Petersburg shrine.[3] That was the real turning point. There would be many more turning points ahead, but on the issue of devotion to God, she would never again waver.

◆ ◆ ◆

Elizabeth never did things in half-measures, and now that she was a Christian, she would go so far as to adopt ascetic practices, so that she would be ever mindful of her dependence on God. For example, during this time, she often wore a heavy belt of lead, which she made herself. "I have bought a thick, heavy lead tube," she wrote in a letter to her mother, "I've flattened it with a hammer and am wearing it under my dress like a belt. All this, to find the Christ. . . ." She began reading books about the lives of saints—to be sure most of the ones she read about outdid her in their ascetic disciplines—and she prayed, often on the cold floor, always asking God to reveal himself to her, to help her live as she should. But at last her love for the poor had found its focus. "I know their only need is Jesus."[4]

In 1914 Elizabeth left St. Petersburg, returning with her daughter Gaiana to her family roots in Anapa on the Black Sea. There she took over running the family estate, a job that required much of her energies and efforts. But even as she was engaged in this mundane work, her faith continued to grow. In her writings of the time, it's clear that she saw herself as something of a prophet, as an instrument of God in the history of Russia. She even seems to have had a sense of her eventual martyrdom. In one poem from this period, she wrote of ancient martyrs who "went forward to their torture freely/as by God's grace shall we as well."[5]

In a letter to Blok from 1916, she said that she wanted "to proclaim the simple word of God."[6] But she understood that serving God meant serving people. "[T]here is no doubt," she wrote some years later, "that the Christian is called to social work." We are "called to organize a better life for the workers, to provide for the old, to build hospitals, care for children, fight against exploitation, injustice, want, lawlessness."[7]

It was the last item on that list that needed combating in 1917, with the violence and turmoil of the Russian Revolution. Elizabeth never excluded involvement in politics as a way of serving God, so she now joined the Socialist Revolutionary Party and in February 1918 was elected deputy mayor of the town. The acting mayor resigned soon thereafter, and Elizabeth became mayor. She spent much of her energies and time protecting her people against the Bolsheviks, who were quickly gaining power. But because all Soviet Marxists applauded any challenge to Tsarist tradition, as a woman mayor she commanded a certain level of respect from them.

In April, Elizabeth traveled to Moscow as an SRP representative.

But by the time she headed home to Anapa in October, full-blown civil war had erupted across the country. Bolshevik guards, including a burly sailor named Sakharov, were stationed on her return train. When word came that enemy soldiers were moving to intercept, Sakharov decided to execute the passengers.

In a brave and brilliant move Elizabeth demanded to first send a telegram to inform Lenin's wife in Moscow of what was happening. Someone produced a form, and Sakharov told her to jot down her message. She handed Sakharov the completed form, and his confidence crumbled as he tapped out the message on the telegraph: "Tell Ulyanova I am to be immediately shot."[8] It was quite a bluff—and it worked. Believing the woman he was about to kill was a friend of Lenin's wife, Sakharov reversed course. In fact, he was so frightened that no one was executed, nor even searched. If the Bolsheviks uncovered the SRP documents in Elizabeth's possession, she would have been executed for sure.

But after arriving safely in Anapa, Elizabeth would need to marshal her courage again. The anti-Bolshevik White Army, which had taken control of the town, wasted no time in arresting her. While the Bolsheviks considered the SRP enemies for not being "Bolshevik" enough, the White Army also considered the SRP enemies for being not "anti-Bolshevik" enough. Elizabeth was caught in the middle. She didn't know what her sentence would be, but death was well within the range of possibilities. What's more, one of the main witnesses for the prosecution was the town's former mayor, who detested Elizabeth and would now have his revenge. But the judge in the trial—a onetime schoolmaster and new acquaintance named Daniel Skobtsov, five years her senior—intervened and saved her life. After the trial, the pair fell in love and married just months later.

The awful civil war between the Red Bolsheviks and the White anti-Bolsheviks raged on, but eventually the Bolsheviks again gained the upper hand in Anapa, forcing thousands to leave. Elizabeth was now well along in her pregnancy with her son Yuri, and for everyone's safety, she had to be separated for a time from her husband. In March 1920 with her mother, Sophia Pilenko, and with her daughter Gaiana, the pregnant Elizabeth boarded an overcrowded steamer bound for Tbilisi, the capital of Georgia, where Yuri was born a month later.

The following year they reunited with Daniel in Constantinople. The city was swamped with refugees so the family eventually made their way north to Belgrade, where Elizabeth gave birth to her third child, a daughter they named Anastasia. As refugees, they were often hungry and sick. Money was hard to come by, and Daniel could never find adequate work. But everyone believed the situation was temporary. As soon as the Bolsheviks were overthrown, the refugees would return. Despite these hopes, however, the years of Bolshevik rule dragged on.

In 1923 Elizabeth and her family settled in Paris, joining a growing community of Russian émigrés struggling for survival. Daniel worked part-time as a teacher, and Liza earned a few francs from sewing, making dolls, and designing stencils for silk scarves. But the many hours of close work damaged her sensitive eyes. Daniel eventually found work as a taxi driver, somewhat improving their situation, but then, during the winter of 1925–26, after years of malnourishment, the entire family came down with influenza.

Everyone recovered in time, except for their little Anastasia—whom they called Nastia. She never seemed to get better and continued to lose weight. The doctors were baffled. Finally, a new physician on the case diagnosed tubercular meningitis. Nastia was admitted immediately to the Pasteur Institute, where for nearly two months Elizabeth stayed by her four-year-old daughter's side. "I feel how all my life my soul has wandered through little, narrow alleys," she wrote at the time. "Now I want a real and cleared path."[9]

The little girl's health continued to falter until, on March 7, she died.

❖ ❖ ❖

The effects of this on the thirty-four-year-old Elizabeth were devastating and life-changing. In the weeks she watched her daughter slipping away, she had rethought everything, and now, when death came, her grief opened up a dramatic new view of the world. "Into the grave's dark maw are plunged all hopes, plans, habits, calculations, and above all, meaning, the whole meaning of life," she later wrote. "In the face of this, everything needs to be re-examined. . . . People call this a visitation of the Lord. A visitation which brings what? Grief? No, more than grief: for he suddenly reveals the true nature of things."[10]

In the death of her beloved Nastia, Elizabeth felt that she had glimpsed once and for all the eternal truth about our existence, and she didn't want ever to slip back into the quotidian concerns of life.

I am convinced that anyone who has shared this experience of eternity, if only once; who has understood which way he is going, if only once; who has perceived the One who precedes him, if only once: such a person will find it hard to deviate from this path, to him all comforts will appear ephemeral, all treasures valueless, all companions superfluous if in their midst he fails to see the one Companion, bearing his cross.[11]

It would be the turning point of her life. She felt God was calling her to a life of ministry to the poor and outcasts among the Russian émigré population. Part of this change in her life had to do with the grim reality that after the death of Nastia, the main bond she shared with her husband, Daniel, had been taken away. Their hasty marriage came with what now seemed like insurmountable differences, and in 1927 the couple separated. Yuri stayed with his father but was free to visit his mother whenever he chose. Gaiana, then fourteen, would remain with her mother.

Elizabeth's writing now took a sharp turn. Practical questions of theology and ministry became her primary focus—and not only in words. She began traveling throughout France for the Russian Student

Christian Movement. The organization was founded in 1923 to help struggling émigrés. While despair manifested among these exiles in rampant alcoholism and suicide, Elizabeth glimpsed Christ in even the most degraded souls. She had the heart of a mother, and many of them bared their souls to her in a way they might never have been able to do with a man, and by seeing their innate dignity, she was able to help them find it again as well.

What she did from day to day and week to week varied considerably. She was often initially invited as a speaker, but once she arrived, the immediate needs of the people would arise and her plans would change. "I would find myself transformed from an official lecturer into a confessor," she said.[12] No task was too small if it meant an opportunity to extend the compassion others desperately needed. She once traveled to the Pyrenees to visit refugees who worked in the mines and lived in horrific squalor. Instead of the talk she intended to give, someone said she should scrub the floor if she really wanted to help. She promptly began doing so. Her humility warmed the atmosphere, and the repentant miners invited her to share a meal. One of the men admitted her kindness forestalled his suicide plans—but only temporarily. Elizabeth would have none of it. She bundled up his things and dragged him to the home of a family she knew. In time the man's hope was reborn.

To some extent, Elizabeth knew that God was calling her simply to share the lives of tramps and outcasts, to show them the love of Christ in a radical way and love them as a mother loves her own children. But she knew this did not mean merely accepting them as they were. To do that would be no better than judging them from on high and making them feel small and unworthy.

No, to truly see the dignity of others and to truly love them meant that love would wage war against the evil that had so terribly harmed them. To do this, she became convinced we must first see in each person a reflection of God himself and respond with the kind of humility and passion to serve that such an awesome revelation requires. As she elaborated in a landmark essay, "The Second Gospel Commandment," only once a person perceives the image of God in his brother

> will yet another mystery be revealed to him, which demands of him his most strenuous struggle, his greatest ascetic ascent. He will see how this image of God is obscured, distorted by an evil power. . . . And in the name of the image of God, darkened by the devil, in the name of love for this image of God that pierces his heart, he will want to begin a struggle with the devil, to become an instrument of God in this terrible and scorching work.[13]

As a mere instrument in the work of restoration and healing, there could be no pride in the labor. She described herself in a poem as the "sword in someone else's hand."[14] She underscored this idea of instrumentality in a slim collection of saints' lives, which she published in 1927. "Her narratives were stylized versions of ancient and already stylized tales," said her biographer, Sergei Hackel. "But she was taking stock of herself in their light."[15]

The death of little Nastia set Elizabeth on a new course, and she would soon do it again. Her growing appreciation for what it meant to give of oneself utterly to this "terrible and scorching work" of redemption was about to radicalize her life even further.

◆ ◆ ◆

A few years after Nastia's death, an opportunity came to move her body to a better location in the cemetery. It was a hard blessing because Elizabeth's presence was legally required for the transfer. To fulfill the duty meant revisiting the death and burial of her beloved daughter in the most concrete terms. But this journey in the necropolis brought another life-changing event. "I became aware of a new and special, broad and all-embracing motherhood," she wrote. "I returned from that cemetery a different person. I saw a new road before me and a new meaning in life." What was it? "To be a mother for all, for all who need maternal care, assistance or protection."[16]

She could no longer be a mother to Nastia, but she would be a mother to everyone she encountered, a mother to the world. But what form would this life take? Elizabeth's only models for such a life were the early Christian monastics. But how could a twice-married mother of three become a nun? Surprisingly, both of her spiritual advisers were open to it. One was Metropolitan Evlogy, who was the Russian Orthodox bishop to much of the Russian diaspora. The other was Father Sergei Bulgakov, whose lectures Elizabeth attended at the Orthodox Theological Institute of Saint Sergius in Paris. In one version of the story, it was actually Evlogy who suggested the move. "I could never be a good nun," said Elizabeth. "I know," answered Evolgy. "But I would like you to be a revolutionary nun."[17]

There were preliminaries. First, her marriage would have to be annulled. This was generally permitted for monastic purposes if both parties agreed, but Daniel Skobtsov was understandably cool to the idea. He nonetheless gave his consent after further conversation with Evlogy, and the couple received an ecclesiastical divorce on March 7, 1932, six years to the day of Nastia's death. Later that month, Elizabeth, dressed all in white, was tonsured and took the monastic habit. Henceforth she would be known as Maria—named for Saint Mary of Egypt, a onetime prostitute whose life became a model of repentance.

Mother Maria began her new life by visiting some monasteries in Latvia and Estonia. But there was a business-as-usual air about these places that she found off-putting. "No one is aware that the world is on fire," she wrote.[18] Given the widening chasm between traditional monasticism and the needs of the world, Maria said there were only two possible responses: "either to deny the new needs of the time without understanding them . . . or, taking this new life into consideration . . . to create a new tradition."[19] Maria chose the second path. She would become the revolutionary nun that Metropolitan Evlogy envisioned.

Mother Maria knew the time for comfort was past and the time to hide from the world was gone. "Today," she said, "there is only monastery for a monk—the whole world. . . . Christ gave the whole world to the Church, and she has no right to renounce its spiritual edification and transfiguration."[20] Thus began a different kind of nun's life, one that would shock some and that would profoundly bless others.

Over the next decade, Maria's principal center would be the homes she established as havens for the destitute and struggling. She rather miraculously procured a desolately empty house at 9 villa de Saxe in Paris and each day providentially brought small additions of furniture and other basics. It was used principally for young Russian women who were without work, and it soon became so crowded that Maria gave up her own room and slept on a cot in the basement, next to the boiler. The large dining space became the common room, where persons of great stature would sometimes come to speak, among them Father Sergei Bulgakov. They converted an upstairs room into a chapel, where Mother Maria's many talents found expression in the icons she painted for the altar partition.

In two years, more space was needed, and the operation was moved to a house that was much larger, and in infinitely worse condition. It was located at 77 rue de Lourmel. In time, Lourmel would become legendary as a place of hospitality, grace, and Christian love. Thousands passed through its doors in the years ahead. They could come and stay as long as necessary, rest, get their bearings, and find healing for soul and body.

In the beginning, Gaiana supervised the kitchen. Mother Maria rose before the sun each morning to go to Les Halles, Paris's massive food market, to bargain for overripe fruit and other food the merchants wished to sell at bargain prices. She would then carry the haul back to Lourmel in a very large sack, and the day's cooking would begin.

Although Lourmel was the principal place of Mother Maria's ministry, she opened other homes too. There was one for single men, another for families who needed accommodation, and there was a capacious country home that served as a sanatorium for consumptives.

◆ ◆ ◆

All she did and how she behaved were without precedent in the world of nuns, and she raised both eyebrows and tempers. She often smoked cigarettes as she shuffled through Les Halles with her giant sack. She dressed shabbily, even for someone who had taken a vow of poverty. Old men's shoes and a second-hand cassock were the usual. But that was only half of it.

A young Anthony Bloom, who many years later became an Orthodox bishop in Britain and Ireland and a popular writer on prayer, was unprepared when he first encountered Mother Maria. "She was a very unusual nun in her behavior and her manners," he said in an interview.

> I was simply staggered when I saw her for the first time in monastic clothes. I was walking along the Boulevard Montparnasse and I saw, in front of a cafe, on the pavement, there was a table, on the table was a glass of beer and behind the glass was sitting a Russian nun in full monastic robes.[21]

Though a stickler at the time, Anthony later became a great admirer of hers.

Mother Maria was aware of her detractors, but she had no doubt she was doing God's will. "At the Last Judgment," she told her friend, Konstantin Mochulsky, "I shall not be asked whether I satisfactorily practiced asceticism, nor how many bows I have made before the divine altar. I will be asked whether I fed the hungry, clothed the naked, visited the sick, and the prisoner in his jail. That is all that will be asked."[22]

Still, her unorthodox ways did not sit well with some in the Russian Orthodox establishment, who made efforts to bring her vision more in line with traditional Orthodox monastic life. In 1936, for instance, a priest, Father Kiprian Kern, arrived from Yugoslavia. His "cold rigorism" caused constant strife and tension with Mother Maria.[23] Her passionate vision of Christian life was calculated to break free of such benumbing shackles, but the break wasn't easy.

Many in the Russian émigré population were also put off by her decidedly untraditional approach. After all, she seemed overly casual about ritual observances, smoked and drank, and had relationships with the most sordid of people. Anyone familiar with the Gospels will hear echoes of the criticisms leveled at Jesus by the religious leaders of his day, and there can be little doubt that Mother Maria reveled in hearing them.

She saw that those who might criticize her as being too worldly were themselves thinking in a worldly way. "The more we go out into the world," she wrote, "the more we give ourselves to the world, the less we are of the world. . . ."[24] But there was no pleasing such critics, and she knew it. "For church circles," she wrote, "we are too far to the left. For the left we are too church-minded."[25] In her radical nonreligious way of serving Christ and her fellow man, she was a picture of what Dietrich Bonhoeffer would a few years hence call "Religionless Christianity."

Maria saw the chaos and the rootlessness of the Russian émigrés as an opportunity to see God anew. "[W]e've become émigrés," she said. "What does that mean? First of all it means freedom." Comfort and convention could become chains. "[W]e must also emigrate out of this well-being," she said. As pilgrims in France, Russian Christians were free to exercise their faith as they liked. But this "weighty gift" of freedom came with obligations. She saw herself and all Christians as charged by God to live out the true faith in action and not to let the dour voices of mere traditionalism quench the fire to serve God by loving and serving others. "We cannot cultivate dead customs—only authentic spiritual fire has weight in religious life. . . . [O]ur God-given freedom calls us to activity and struggle." The struggle would be difficult, but it came with its own rewards. "[W]e will become fools [for] Christ, because we know not only the difficulty of this path but also the immense happiness of feeling God's hand upon what we do."[26]

She saw Christians as coworkers with God. Success would depend upon God's will, she said, but believers nonetheless had their divinely appointed part to play. "[E]ach of us," she said, "is faced with the demand to strain all our forces, not fearing the most difficult endeavor, in ascetic self-restraint, giving our souls for others sacrificially and lovingly, to follow in Christ's footsteps to our appointed Golgotha."[27]

She exemplified grace taken to the extreme. Some thought she took it too far. She once moved a young addict into the house. Right away the girl stole twenty-five francs from Gaiana. While there was no proof, Gaiana demanded she get the boot. Instead, Maria stashed the same amount behind a couch cushion and made a public display of finding it there. "[T]he money was not stolen, after all," she said. "It is dangerous to make an accusation without investigating," she warned.[28] The girl was undone by Maria's unwarranted kindness.

One of the greatest ironies of her life is that although she felt called by God to be a mother to the world, all three of the children she bore would die young. Nastia had died at age four. At twenty-one, Gaiana married and returned to Russia to be with her husband. Her many letters home were full of joy, but in July 1936 Maria received word of Gaiana's death from typhus. She was only twenty-two. Maria, stunned by the news, bolted into the street and didn't return until late in the day, after which she secluded herself for a month to mourn. To lose Gaiana just ten years after losing her Nastia was an earth-shattering blow. "A black night of the utmost spiritual loneliness," she described it.[29] There was no possibility of returning to Russia for herself, so Maria had to make do with a memorial service in Paris. She prayed face down on the floor the entire service. She had dreams of Gaiana and expressed her grief in more poems.

In 1937, Mother Maria was growing more restless and more radical than ever. Combatting her sorrows, she abandoned herself to service, sometimes going for a full day without food and sleep. She would occasionally disappear for days at a time, seeking out homeless sufferers wherever they were, sharing in their existence and inviting them to return to the house at 77 rue de Lourmel for a cheap meal and company. "My feeling for them all is maternal. I would like to swaddle them and rock them to sleep."[30]

◆ ◆ ◆

In 1939 the Second World War broke out over Europe. In August, Hitler invaded Poland, and with lightning speed the Nazi juggernaut swept eastward toward Russia and westward toward France. On June 14, 1940, Paris fell to the Germans, and life changed dramatically. A mass exodus made refugees of more than two-thirds of the city's population, while those remaining lived under ever-tightening Nazi control.

The German takeover provided an unlikely opportunity for Maria and her ex-husband to reconcile. Their son Yuri lived between their homes. Working with his mother during the day, he would return at night to sleep at his father's house. The practice was too risky to continue, so Daniel recommended he temporarily stay at Lourmel until things settled down. For a brief period the three again lived together under the same roof, though mom and dad had disagreements about their boy's future. Yuri, a student at the Sorbonne, was considering ordination. Mom was for it, dad against. Little did anyone know how much was riding on this question.

Of course, the greatest and most pressing risks belonged to the Jews. Maria had Jewish friends with a farm outside of Paris. Worried the Nazis would seize the property, they transferred the title to Daniel, and he left Lourmel to manage the farm. Meanwhile, Yuri stayed with his mother and assumed a greater role in the ministry—which increasingly included resisting the Occupation.

Mother Maria and her brothers and sisters in Christ at Lourmel were not for a moment tempted to go along with Nazi rule in Paris. They knew that as Christians, they must work with the French Resistance to do all they could—and of course, this meant helping the Jews of Paris. She was one of those rare Christians who saw that the fate of the Jews and Christians, indeed all of humanity, were inextricably intertwined.

It all went back to her understanding of the idea that humanity bears the distorted image of God and the mission of Christ to restore that image. The Jews had a special historical role to play in that story. "God faces His image and likeness, His chosen people, Israel, which represents . . . the person of any people," she wrote. "Throughout its ancient history Israel, in a certain sense, was bearing God. One had to have been a person for the absolute Person to become incarnate in one."[31] So as she saw it, an attack on the Jews was an attack on personhood itself, on the image of God in all people. To defend the Jews was to defend all of humanity, all of what makes us human. But Maria's understanding was not mere theory. As the Nazis increased their persecution of the Parisian Jews, it became life-and-death reality.

In March 1942, Adolf Eichmann ordered that all Jews in occupied territories must wear the yellow star of David. The day of this decree, Mother Maria wrote an unsigned five-stanza poem that quickly spread across all of Paris. The opening and closing lines run as follows:

> *Two triangles, King David's star.*
> *No insult, this ancestral blazon.*
> *It indicates a noble way.*
> *It marks a chosen nation.*

> *May you, stamped by this seal,*
> *this star of David, by decree,*
> *in your constrained response, reveal*
> *that you are spiritually free.*[32]

It was clear that the Christians at Lourmel would not lie down in the face of the Nazi evil. The number of Jews hidden at Lourmel and Mother Maria's other houses cannot be counted. Maria and her colleagues did all they could to hide them and then to transport them to safety beyond France. The facilities were already crammed beyond capacity, but the need just grew.

In her fearlessness and defiance, she seemed to have made her peace with death. At one point, Mother Maria remarked that it was a miracle the Germans hadn't come to Lourmel. If they did, she had a plan. "If the Germans come looking for Jews," she once said, "I'll show them the icon of the Mother of God."[33] Eventually when the Nazis did come to Lourmel—to hang recruitment posters, not arrest Jews—Maria promptly tore the posters down.

There was nothing of the diplomat in her. At one point she met several times with a German pastor named Peters, who was interested in her Christian social work, but when she found out he was a proud Nazi and part of the Nazified "Deutsche Christen"[34] she challenged him: "How could you be both a Christian and a Nazi?"[35]

The year prior to the Nazi occupation, in October 1939, Father Dimitri Klepinin had come to Lourmel, replacing Father Kiprian Kern. As much as Father Kiprian and Mother Maria bumped heads and antagonized each other, Father Dimitri and she saw eye to eye. His friendship would be a profound comfort to her and to her son Yuri and the others at Lourmel. Father Dimitri was a mild-mannered and sensitive soul, but on this issue of what to do in the face of Nazi evil, he was clear and bold. He would joyfully lie to the Nazis and deceive them in any way necessary. After the Eichmann decree, many Jews came to Lourmel requesting forged baptismal certificates, and at the risk of his own life, Father Dimitri began producing them by the dozens. "I think the good Christ would give me that paper if I were in their place," he said.[36] To cover these tracks, in case the Nazis checked church rolls, he began forging the names of Jews into the congregational records of Lourmel.

On July 15–16, 1942, things took a sharp turn for the worse when the Nazis began mass arrests of the Jews. Nearly 13,000 were rounded up. Of those, 6,900 were taken to the Vélodrome d'Hiver; 4,051 were children. The enclosed sports stadium was a brief walk from Lourmel, and Mother Maria went to see what she could do to help. The guard at the entrance was French. To him Maria was any other nun—how much trouble could a nun cause? So after telling her to restrict herself to spiritual work, he let her pass.

What she saw inside was horrific. There were just ten latrines, and only a single hydrant provided water on a blazing summer day. Mother Maria did all she could to comfort those who were there and distributed the little food she was able to bring. She ministered amid this chaos for three days. Seizing an opportunity with some sympathetic garbage collectors, she helped smuggle four children out of the Vélodrome over two days in a pair of trash cans. At least these four were saved. At the end of the five days, every child in the stadium was taken from its parents and sent to Auschwitz, where—in one of the most evil acts of an evil regime—all four thousand were murdered.

After Christmas, rumors came that the Gestapo and the feared SD security force had their eyes on Maria and Father Dimitri and that arrests were likely. The pair had already been interviewed by a plainclothes SD officer named Hans Hoffmann in August and knew that he was keeping a dossier on their suspected activities. Friends advised they go underground. Daniel urged Maria to hide at the farm. She and Yuri had recently begun visiting him, and it was far enough out of town that she might escape notice. But she pushed off all concerns. "Only have faith," she said.[37]

◆ ◆ ◆

At last Yuri decided to enter the priesthood. Metropolitan Evlogy supported the idea, but the boy's father was a different matter. Unfortunately, the persuasive bishop could not help this time. Maria decided to travel to the farm on Sunday, February 7, 1943, to convince her ex-husband the move was right for their son. As she planned it, Yuri would arrive on Monday and then talk with Daniel directly. He never arrived.

On February 8, 1943, Hoffmann and two Gestapo agents came

to Lourmel for Mother Maria. When told she was away, they began searching and seizing her files. Yuri was trying to leave to warn his mother when he was spotted by Hoffmann and searched. In his jacket pocket they found a letter written to Father Dimitri requesting a baptismal certificate. They would hold Yuri as a hostage until Maria came to see them. Many hostages of the Nazis were being shot, so the stakes were high.

The Gestapo took Father Dimitri as well and interrogated him for six hours. Hoffmann offered freedom if he agreed to stop helping Jews. "I am a Christian," he answered, "and must act as I must."[38] Hoffmann called him a Jew-lover and struck his face. Bold as Mother Maria, Father Dimitri lifted his pectoral cross and asked, "And this Jew here, do you know Him?"[39] That time he was knocked to the ground. But the Christians in Mother Maria's orbit would not compromise their faith. For them it was unthinkable. They had all made their peace with death.

Mother Maria's own mother, Sophia Pilenko, now in her eighties, was no different. Mother Maria got word of Yuri's arrest late Monday and cautiously returned to Paris on Wednesday to immediate arrest. Hoffmann taunted Sophia. "You brought your daughter up badly!" he shouted. "All she can do is help yids!" But the old woman replied, "My daughter is a genuine Christian. . . . If you were threatened by some disaster, she would help you too."[40] Mother Maria smiled and agreed. In this way they heaped hot coals on the heads of their persecutors.

Maria was first taken to the Gestapo headquarters in Paris, where Yuri and Father Dimitri were being held. Daniel tried to get help from lawyers, anyone who could secure their release, but it was useless. Together at first, the prisoners were separated later in the month. Yuri and Father Dimitri were taken to Compiègne-Royallieu, where the Nazis had established an internment camp. Mother Maria was left behind until April. Daniel tried to visit her on April 21 but only caught sight of her on a bus being transferred to Compiègne. She waved as she passed.

Briefly reunited at Compiègne, Maria saw her son for the last time.

Yuri snuck through a window to be with her. They spent a few hours together and said their good-byes at dawn. Maria told him not to fret about her. She knew that her son's faith was strong. While they were together, Yuri told his mother that his favorite prayer was the Jesus Prayer: "Lord Jesus Christ, Son of God, have mercy on me a sinner." Regardless of their circumstances, he said, this mutual prayer would hold them together.

The following morning, Maria was sealed with two hundred other women into cattle trucks to make the long journey east. They were in these trucks without sanitation or water for three days. Eventually they arrived at Ravensbrück Concentration Camp. She would spend two years there.

Yuri and Father Dimitri remained at Compiègne through 1943, making the best of circumstances by holding church, Bible study, and even some frivolity. Father Dimitri was able to write letters to his wife and told in one how he, Yuri, and two others were going to save the wine they were served with lunch and drink it together before a party planned to boost prisoner morale. It didn't do much good. On December 16, Yuri and Father Dimitri were transferred from Compiègne to Buchenwald and then moved again to Dora. Ten days after his arrival, Yuri's body erupted in boils. The Nazis had no plans to treat the condition. The twenty-four-year-old Yuri was instead dispatched on February 6, 1944. Father Dimitri joined him just days later, succumbing to pneumonia.

◆ ◆ ◆

Mother Maria was the same beacon in Ravensbrück that she was in Paris. In the midst of horrifically depressing conditions, she organized prayer groups in the evenings. She read from the Gospels, and then everyone discussed the meaning of what they'd heard, and then they prayed together. Well-read and knowledgeable on many subjects, Maria organized discussion groups to help her fellow prisoners get their minds off the misery of the camp. After visits with her, one survivor recalled, prisoners left "radiant."[41]

Some of the Russian prisoners worked during the day in fields that were outside the camp, and when they returned they sometimes gave Mother Maria a potato or a carrot that they had smuggled back under their clothing. Mother Maria rarely ate these herself but put them in a secret place to share later with those she felt needed them more than she did. It was only in the end, when she was herself ailing, that she would indulge herself.

During her two years at Ravensbrück, Mother Maria was able to do some embroidery. The only one that survived is an extraordinary visualization of the Normandy Invasion stitched with foraged materials on a kerchief and patterned on the Bayeaux tapestry. She had bet someone that the Russians would win the war before the Allies had a chance to enact their D-day plans. But she was wrong, and she happily paid up in the form of this beautiful piece of art.

Another survivor remembered her as constantly upbeat and friendly. "She was never downcast, never," said Solange Périchon. "She allowed nothing of secondary importance to impede her contact with people."[42]

But despite her buoyant spirit, conditions in the camp deteriorated, and the overcrowding, disease, and malnutrition took their toll. In January 1945, her health was suffering, so she accepted the camp's offer of a pink card given to those who wished to be excused from the work details. Like all such offers by the Nazis, it was no offer at all. Soon all those who held such cards were transported to another camp, which was a place designed to accelerate death. The Nazis knew they were losing the war and wished to kill off as many of these prisoners as they could. Amazingly, Maria survived five weeks at that camp and then was for some reason returned to the regular camp, where she lived out her last days.

Though she was unable to stand for roll call, she traded some bread for thread so she could embroider one last icon. Survivors said she was constantly at prayer now. This embroidery would be her final litany. It depicted Mary holding Jesus, a traditional image, but in Mother Maria's rendition Mary held Christ crucified. She never had the chance to finish it.[43]

We do not know the details of her last moments. On March 30, 1945, Mother Maria Skobtsova was taken to the gas chamber at Ravensbrück. It was Good Friday. Some have said she was selected to die, but others say she deliberately took the place of another prisoner who had been chosen to die. "It is very possible that she took the place of a frantic companion," said survivor Jacqueline Péry. "It would have been entirely in keeping with her generous life. In any case she offered herself consciously to the holocaust . . . thus assisting each one of us to accept the cross. . . ." Péry added, "She radiated the peace of God."[44]

She died the next day, on Great and Holy Saturday, a paradoxical day on the church calendar when Orthodox Christians mark both Christ's Sabbath rest in the tomb from his labor on the cross *and* his violent destruction of hades and the liberation of its captives.

◆ ◆ ◆

According to Jim Forest, writing in the introduction to Mother Maria's essential writings in English, the reason Mother Maria was not canonized by the Orthodox church until the twenty-first century was likely that she heroically and uncompromisingly challenged a church hierarchy that had allowed the church of Jesus Christ to become ossified by traditionalism and to abandon its holy and prophetic witness against the world around it.

Mother Maria remains an indictment of any form of Christianity that seeks Christ chiefly inside the walls of our churches. Like so many who have valiantly served God, she challenged the church establishment even when not wishing to do so. Her passion for God lived out in her time and place enabled others to see God anew, shorn of religious trappings. Father Michael Plekon wrote that Mother Maria's life points us to a fundamental reality . . . namely that the Christian's commitment is not primarily to a heritage, to structures of the past nor even to visions of the what the future should be. Rather, each Christian, monastic or cleric or layperson, is called to real life, life in the Church and the world as we find it, an encounter with God, oneself, and the neighbor in need.[45]

But the Orthodox Church's hesitation to canonize this great woman of God was eventually seen for what it was: a mistake. Finally in 2004, on May 1 and 2, Mother Maria would become Saint Maria of Paris. At the Saint Alexander Nevsky Cathedral in Paris, just three miles from 77 rue de Lourmel, she—along with her son Yuri and Father Dimitri Klepinin—were officially recognized as saints in the Orthodox Church by the Holy Synod of the Patriarchate of Constantinople. July 20 was established as the day each year when they would be remembered in the church calendar. Another distinction came even earlier from the Jewish people she sought to save. In 1985 Yad Vashem listed Mother Maria and Father Dimitri as Righteous Gentiles for their sacrificial efforts.[46]

Just as Dietrich Bonhoeffer prophetically challenged the Lutheran Church of Germany in his time, so Mother Maria challenged the Orthodox Church of hers. Both understood that to serve Jesus Christ with all one's heart, soul, mind, and body—that is to be the church of Jesus Christ, to be the Bride for which he will one day return.

Even so, come Lord Jesus.

FIVE
Corrie ten Boom

1892-1983

M any people know the inspiring story of Corrie ten Boom and her family, who risked their lives to rescue their Jewish neighbors during the Nazi occupation of Holland. Their saga is captured beautifully in Corrie's classic book *The Hiding Place*, as well as in the 1975 film of the same name, starring the great Julie Harris. But few people are aware of the larger story that led the family to hide Jews in their home in the first place. It was a bold and tremendously fateful decision, as we shall see.

The family's bravery didn't come out of nowhere. It grew out of a profound Christian faith of a family who had for three generations devoutly believed that the Jews were God's chosen people. Like Lutheran pastor and theologian Dietrich Bonhoeffer in Germany, they believed it was their duty as Christians to help God's chosen people when their lives were in danger, as they certainly were in Nazi-occupied Holland in the 1940s.

The same faith that led to the Ten Boom family's determination to help as many Jews as possible also led to Corrie's great ministry in the decades after the war: teaching people how to forgive even the most horrific sins committed against them.

◆ ◆ ◆

Cornelia "Corrie" ten Boom was born on April 15, 1892, in Amsterdam. She was the youngest of the four children born to her parents, Casper and Cornelia. Corrie's brother, Willem, was born in 1886; her sister, Arnolda "Nollie" was born in 1890; and Elizabeth "Betsie" was born in 1885.

Casper ten Boom was a watchmaker, just as his own father had been. The family watch shop had opened for business in 1837, in a narrow Haarlem house called the Beje (a shortened version of the street address, the Barteljorisstraat), where generations of Ten Booms had lived.

Already nearly a century before the Nazi invasion of Holland, we see the first sign that the Ten Boom family had a special commitment to the welfare of their Jewish neighbors. It happened when Corrie's grandfather Willem received a visit from the family minister, Dominee Witteveen.

"Willem," the minister had begun, "you know the Scriptures tell us to pray for the peace of Jerusalem and the blessing of the Jews."

"Yes, Dominee," Willem responded. "I have always loved God's ancient people—they gave us our Bible and our Savior."

Shortly after this, the two men formed a prayer fellowship for the express purpose of praying for the Jews. "In a divine way which is beyond human understanding," Corrie wrote, "God answered those prayers. It was in the same house, exactly one hundred years later, that Grandfather's son, my father, four of his grandchildren, and one great-grandson were arrested for helping save the lives of Jews during the German occupation of Holland."[1]

After Corrie's parents married in 1884, they moved to a house in the Jewish quarter of Amsterdam, about twelve miles from Haarlem. There Casper opened a jewelry store. He was a member of the Dutch Reformed Church, but his Jewish neighbors, sensing his openness and friendliness toward them, often invited him to take part in their Sabbaths and other holy days and study the Talmud with them. Corrie said that he was "given opportunities to understand and explain the fulfillment of the prophecies of the Old Testament in the New Testament."² Casper's love for the Jewish people increased during those years.

Shortly after Corrie's birth, her paternal grandfather died, so Casper and Cornelia moved the family back to Haarlem to take over the watch shop. Despite modest circumstances, the small house above the Beje was a deeply happy one, and gratitude to God that grew out of their deep faith was at the center of their happiness. Their home actually comprised two tall, narrow houses that had been turned into one. Neighbors frequently turned up for meals in the Ten Boom house, where they were welcomed enthusiastically. The conversation was lively, and family concerts often followed.

Faith was at the heart of everything for the Ten Boom's. Corrie's mother led five-year-old Corrie to belief in Jesus Christ, after which the little girl immediately began praying for the people on her street, especially for the drunks she often saw being led into jail.

Corrie's mother taught her children to have compassion for those whose minds or bodies were damaged. Her father's painstaking work repairing watches showed Corrie the importance of working hard and doing one's best. He urged his children to live out their faith and to live lives of honesty and integrity, recognizing that God's eyes were always on them.

Each day opened and closed in Bible-reading and prayer, and throughout her long life, Corrie never forgot how her father came into her room at night to tuck her in—to pray with her, touch her face, and wish her a good night. Some forty years later, while trying to sleep in a filthy concentration camp bed, she would remember the comforting feel of her father's hand on her face. Many of the experiences and Scripture lessons their parents gave Corrie and Betsie as children prepared them for what was at the time an unimaginable future.

It seemed that everyone in Haarlem knew and loved Casper ten Boom. He was known affectionately as the Grand Old Man of Haarlem. Each day after lunch it was his habit to walk through the town exchanging greetings with his friends.

Corrie's three aunts lived with the family too. They were devout in their faith as well. Corrie recalled how her Tante Anna formed a club for female servants of wealthy families, inviting them to the Beje in the evenings for sewing, embroidery, singing, and Bible lessons; and Tante Jans organized get-togethers for young women and invited soldiers to the Ten Boom home for evenings of friendly home life and Bible study.

Through the years the special family commitment to the welfare of the Jewish people continued. In fact, Corrie's brother Willem believed God was calling him to serve as a minister to the Jews. He traveled to Germany for study in the 1920s, and in 1927, just six years before the Third Reich came to power, he wrote a thesis in which he declared that (in reference to the Jewish people) the "severest pogrom in the entire history of the world could come in Germany."[3] At the time, his professors laughed at the idea, which they thought preposterous.

As the First World War came to an end, the Ten Boom family wanted to reach out to the defeated nation of Germany, where large numbers of children were suffering from malnutrition. Corrie's father contacted watchmaker colleagues all over the Netherlands, suggesting that they take in a German child or two, feed them well and get them healthy, and then return them to their families. Many agreed to do so. The Ten Boom family took in four such children.

In 1920, when Corrie was twenty-eight, she began attending a Haarlem Bible school, studying the Old and New Testaments, church history, ethics, and dogmatics. The following year Corrie lost her mother, who had suffered several strokes and become bedridden. It was around this time that Corrie, who had always been responsible for the housekeeping, began helping her father in his shop, assisting customers, keeping the books, and eventually learning how to repair watches herself. Corrie took to the family business so readily that her father decided to send her to Switzerland, so that she could learn the craft properly. She would become the first woman in the Netherlands to be licensed as a watchmaker.

Corrie's brother, Willem, and sister Nollie eventually married and had families of their own, but Corrie and Betsie remained single. In 1923, as a way of sharing their Christian faith, the sisters began forming clubs for young girls. In those days Sunday school typically ended when girls were about twelve, but Corrie and Betsie wanted to provide girls with further religious education during the critical teenage years. They began a walking club and, after many of their hikes, would take some of the girls to a youth church. The club became so popular that within a short time, Corrie and Betsie recruited dozens of other leaders to assist them. After a clubhouse was donated the sisters formed a number of clubs, some for teaching English, others for gymnastics, music, and hiking. But each of them included Bible study. As a result, many of the young girls came to faith.

Eventually, Corrie started a club for boys and girls together. Coeducation was virtually unheard of at the time, and some church leaders and many parents were shocked. But Corrie knew some of the girls in the clubs were meeting boyfriends in secret. She felt that a club, where they could meet openly and under friendly supervision, would be a healthier situation. And so it proved to be.

Corrie's zeal to share her faith seemed to know no bounds. While all the clubs continued to thrive, she began holding religious services for children with intellectual challenges. "[I]t was such a joy," she wrote, "to know that the Lord doesn't need a high IQ in a person in order to reveal Himself. In fact, people of normal or superior intelligence likewise need the help of the Holy Spirit to understand the spiritual truths, which are only spiritually discerned."[4] Corrie had also befriended a mentally disturbed woman in a hospital and visited her often, sharing her faith with her.

By the early 1930s Corrie's three aunts had died, and the population of the Beje was down to Corrie, Betsie, and their father. But the quiet did not last long. The Ten Booms soon agreed to take in seven children of missionaries, who were working abroad. The children much preferred the friendly environment of the Ten Boom home to the cold atmosphere of a boarding school.

This period was especially joyful for Corrie and Betsie. Nearly fifty years later Corrie recalled, "Our quiet, thin little three-story house was suddenly stretching its walls and echoing with the activity of [the] children. The side door swung in and out like the pendulum on one of our clocks, and it was a good sound. . . . Although Betsie and I never married, we received such love from all of our children and were able to give them so much of ours!"[5]

During these years, Corrie was constantly in prayer, asking God to help her meet the needs—particularly the financial needs—of her large family. And she taught her foster children much about God. It was not until many years later, following the war, that Corrie learned how deeply her teaching about God, and the need to forgive our enemies, had sunk into these children.

By 1940 all seven children were grown and gone, and another, darker, phase of Corrie's life was about to begin. She never forgot the night of May 14, when Adolf Hitler ordered "the first large-scale airborne attack in the history of warfare" on the citizens of Rotterdam, less than thirty miles from Haarlem.[6] These attacks killed close to nine hundred people, mostly civilians. Thousands more were wounded, and seventy-eight thousand were rendered homeless.

That night Corrie, awakening in terror to the sounds of bombs landing and sirens screaming, learned the first of many lessons in forgiveness from her beloved sister. In addition to praying that night for their country, the injured, and the dead, Betsie was also praying "for the Germans, up there in the planes, caught in the first of the giant evil loose in Germany."[7] Corrie, hearing her sister's prayers, prayed that God would hear Betsie's prayers, because she could not bring herself to pray for the Germans. Just five days later, when the Nazis threatened Holland with another horrific air attack, the Dutch surrendered. Soon German tanks rumbled down the streets where Corrie had played as a child.

Holland suddenly became an occupied country. But the work for which God had spent fifty years preparing Corrie was about to begin.

❖ ❖ ❖

The German occupation brought many changes to the Ten Boom family. Their telephone was cut off, their bicycles were confiscated, and everyone was issued an identity card. They needed ration cards to buy food. Throughout the country young men walking with their families on a Sunday afternoon, or merely sitting with them in church, were arrested and taken to Germany to work in factories. Many never returned.

The Nazis demanded that everyone turn in his radio. The Ten Booms had two, so they turned in one and then built a special hiding place beneath the staircase for the other. This way they could listen to news of the war from England.

Back at the watch shop, Corrie and her father now found themselves serving German soldiers. At night the family lay awake listening to dogfights between British and German planes in the skies over Haarlem.

Things gradually grew worse for Holland's Jews. Eventually they were required to wear yellow stars on their clothes, and eighty-year-old Casper, identifying with God's ancient people as he always had, decided to wear one too. Rocks were thrown at Jewish-owned businesses; anti-Semitic words were painted on synagogues; and signs were posted on stores announcing that Jews would not be served. All these things were the work of a pro-Nazi Dutch organization known as the National Socialist Bond. While some joined the NSB for more food, clothing coupons, and better jobs and housing, others did so because they truly believed in the Nazi cause.

Gradually Jewish shops were closed, and Jewish homes emptied of their inhabitants. Nobody knew where they had gone. Had they gone into hiding, or had the Gestapo taken them away?

Corrie's brother, Willem, had been bravely hiding Jews since the occupation began, both in his own home and in the homes of others. It took a terrifying incident to lead Corrie and Betsie to do the same. In November 1941 Corrie saw four German soldiers march to the store belonging to her neighbor, Mr. Weil. Moments later Mr. Weil emerged, a gun muzzle pressed to his stomach. Leaving him outside, the German soldier rejoined the others to smash everything breakable and to steal the fur coats Mr. Weil sold in his store.

Corrie and Betsie urged their friend to come into their house before the Germans could take him away. They contacted Willem, who instructed his son Kik to take Mr. Weil and his wife away to safety.

This launched Corrie's work with the underground resistance movement. But as she considered what continuing in this work would involve—lying, stealing, perhaps even killing—she had to ask herself if this was how God wanted her to behave in such circumstances. How should Christians act in the face of evil?

One evening, her mind made up, Corrie prayed, "Lord Jesus, I offer myself for Your people. In any way. Any place, Any time."[8] Since increasing numbers of Jews were being arrested on the streets, Corrie started traveling to the homes of the family's Jewish customers.

One night a knock came on the alley door. A frightened woman stood in the darkness. "My name is Kleermaker. I'm a Jew," she told Corrie. She had heard that the Ten Booms had helped another Jew. Casper ten Boom did not let her finish. "In this household, God's people are always welcome."[9]

Two nights later another knock came, and Corrie answered the door to an elderly Jewish couple. They joined Mrs. Kleermaker upstairs.

CORRIE TEN BOOM

Two years into the Nazi occupation, the food shortage was becoming acute. Ration cards were not issued to Jews, so the Ten Booms used their own to purchase food for their Jewish guests. It was becoming urgently necessary to obtain more cards however they could. How else would they feed their Jewish guests—and any future guests they might receive?

A name popped into Corrie's head: Fred Koornstra, the father of a girl who attended the religious services Corrie held for the intellectually challenged. Koornstra now worked at the Food Office, where ration books were issued.

Praying that God would close her lips if Fred could not be trusted, Corrie told him they had some unexpected guests—Jewish guests. They needed ration cards. Could he help? Fred was sympathetic. But he told Corrie he could not give her extra ration cards because they were checked in too many ways. The only way to get their hands on extra cards would be to stage a robbery. He knew of a man who might cooperate in this effort. How many ration cards did Corrie need?

Corrie, intending to answer "five," instead found herself saying "one hundred." A week later Fred knocked on the Ten Booms's doors and handed them one hundred ration cards. He would continue to bring cards each week. Since even sympathetic Hollanders, due to their limited resources, were reluctant to take on extra people on their limited resources, these precious cards meant the Jews living with the Ten Booms, and those who came after them, could find safer homes farther away from the center of Haarlem.

Trust was the issue, but as writer and minister Michal Ann Goll wrote,

In a social and political environment in which the wisest human course was to trust no one, it nevertheless was necessary on occasion for Corrie to seek help from someone who could supply a particular need. The risk was in not knowing whether the person approached would be sympathetic or would betray the operation to the Nazi authorities. Time after time Corrie received what she called the "gift of knowledge" when these decisions were needed.[10]

There would be other problems to solve—women who went into labor, for instance. Since the Ten Booms knew so many people in Haarlem, asking for help would not be a problem, except for the ticklish fact that they did not know the political views of all their neighbors. Who would help deliver a Jewish baby in secret—and who would turn the mother in?

The only solution was to pray. They had no doubt that God was real and that he wanted them to continue doing what they were doing. They knew if they prayed he would guide them.

At a gathering of underground workers, a well-known architect suggested that Corrie allow him to design a secret room in her house, just in case the Gestapo paid an unexpected visit. He chose Corrie's bedroom at the top of the house, and within days he and his workmen had constructed a brick wall, creating a two-and-a-half-foot-wide space big enough for several people to hide in. A low, sliding panel gave access to the hiding place. The secret room contained a mattress, a bucket of water, vitamins, and hardtack. The Gestapo, the architect predicted, would never find the secret room.

Over the next few months scores of Jews passed through the Ten Boom home, staying for as little as one night or as long as several weeks. Corrie and Betsie found innovative ways to deal with all sorts of problems, such as getting their telephone line reinstalled—a great help now that Corrie was working with some eighty underground volunteers.

The sisters developed a code when talking on the telephone, which they knew might be tapped. "We have a woman's watch here that needs repairing. But I can't find a mainspring. Do you know who might have one?" This meant, "We have a Jewish woman in need of a hiding place, and we can't find one among our regular contacts."[11]

Finally the day came when the Ten Booms began taking in permanent guests—seven in all. A member of the underground installed an alarm system, and the refugees began holding regular drills to see how quickly they could make it to the hiding place at the top of the house.

Even with the shortages and the stress and strains of daily life, the Ten Booms and their guests were cheerful. Corrie and Betsie did their best to keep their guests entertained, performing little concerts in the evenings or reading Shakespeare plays aloud. Their Jewish guests also helped pass the time in the evenings with Hebrew lessons.

Eighteen months after they had begun actively helping Jews, the Beje had become "the center of an underground ring that spread to the farthest corners of Holland. Here daily came dozens of workers, reports, appeals," Corrie wrote. "We had to go on, but we knew that disaster could not be long in coming. . . ."[12]

The first blow struck at Nollie's house. Corrie's sister and the Jews hiding in her home were arrested. While the Jews were freed shortly afterward in a daring rescue operation, Nollie remained behind bars for seven weeks.

And then, on February 28, 1944, Betsie woke Corrie, who was sick with influenza. Betsie said that a man was downstairs waiting to speak with her. The man—a stranger—told Corrie his wife had been arrested, and that he needed six hundred guilders to bribe a policeman. Corrie hesitated, not liking the way the man refused to meet her eyes. But in the end, fearing a Jewish life was at stake, she told him to come back in half an hour for the money.

After sending an underground worker to the bank, Corrie went back to bed and fell asleep. Suddenly she was awakened by the sound of the ringing buzzer, running feet, and terrified voices. One by one, the "permanent guests" raced into Corrie's room and slid through the little door to the secret room.

Moments later, a man burst into Corrie's bedroom and began firing questions at her. "So you're the ringleader! Tell me now, where are you hiding the Jews."

"I don't know what you're talking about," Corrie responded.[13]

The man, a member of the Gestapo, ordered Corrie to dress and

escorted her downstairs, where her father, Betsie, and several underground workers were waiting. Other Gestapo agents were banging on
the walls with hammers, searching for secret rooms.

An agent turned his attention to Corrie, determined to find out
information. He slapped her hard across the face. "Where are the Jews?"
he demanded. "Where do you hide the ration cards?" He slapped her
again and again. "Where is your secret room?"

Corrie, about to lose consciousness from the beating, cried out,
"Lord Jesus, protect me!"

The Gestapo agent's hand stopped in mid-slap. "If you say that
name again, I'll kill you!" he shouted. But he did not slap her again.[14]

As other underground workers knocked on the shop door, the
Gestapo ordered them into the house and began interrogating them
too. Eventually Corrie, her father, brother Willem, sisters Betsie and
Nollie, along with Nollie's son, Peter, were taken to the police station,
along with thirty-five others who happened to stop by the Beje that day.

That evening, after hours of being asked for their names, addresses,
and occupations, many prisoners gathered around Casper ten Boom
to hear him pray the words from Psalm 119:114, 117: "You are my hiding place and my shield; I hope in Your word. . . . Hold me up, and I
shall be safe."

The next morning the Ten Boom family—Corrie, Betsie, Willem,
Nollie, Peter, and Casper—were marched outside and ordered onto a
bus. Two hours later they arrived in The Hague and were brought to
a building rumored to be the Gestapo headquarters in Holland. They
spent another long day answering the same questions, over and over
again, and then they were ordered into an army truck to be driven to
Scheveningen, where a brick-walled federal penitentiary awaited them.

After a long wait the women prisoners were ordered to follow a
matron down a corridor. Turning for what would be her last look at her
beloved father, Corrie burst out, "Father! God be with you!"

Casper turned to face her. "And with you, my daughters," he said.[15]

Down the corridor first Betsie, then Nollie, then Corrie were put into tiny cells. As the door opened to Corrie's cell, she saw four women already there, one on a cot, three others on straw ticking on the floor. A kind cell mate hung up her hat. This prison was to be her home for the next four months. Food was handed in through a shelf in the door, as was a sanitary bucket.

Intense boredom settled in, relieved only by Corrie's worry over her family and the fate of the little group of people hiding on the top floor of the Beje, which was now surrounded by Germans day and night.

Two weeks later the door to the cell opened, and a matron ordered Corrie out. She was led along another prison corridor and put into another cell. The matron slammed the door behind her and left. She was now in solitary confinement, with only a stinking cot and blanket to keep her company. No explanation was given. When food was shoved through the shelf in the door, she was too sick to get up. Some time later a hunk of bread was thrown in where she could reach it. In her fear, she remembered finding it difficult to pray. On April 17 she was allowed her first shower in six weeks. She was deeply grateful for small mercies.

On Hitler's birthday, all the guards attended a party. The inmates took full advantage of the sudden freedom and shouted messages to one another. Thus Corrie received a message from Betsie—"God is good"—and discovered that Nollie had been released a month previously.[16] So had her brother, Willem, and nephew Peter. Corrie was overjoyed. But what had become of her father?

A week later Corrie received a package from Nollie, filled with cookies, a sweater, a towel, and a needle and thread. There was also a message under the stamp on the envelope: "All the watches in your closet are safe."[17] Understanding the real meaning of this, Corrie burst into tears of joy.

But on May 3 there was devastating news. Nollie wrote a letter to Corrie telling her that their father, Casper ten Boom, had survived only ten days in prison.

Not long afterward Corrie was called to her first hearing. The officer treated her kindly, using every psychological tool he had to break her down and get her to admit to illegal activities. But she stood firm—and then, to her own astonishment, she began to tell him about God. The officer swiftly cut her off, but the next day, and for two additional days afterward, he had her taken out of her cell and asked her to tell him more about what the Bible taught and about her family, especially her father.

The German confessed to Corrie that he could not bear the work he did at the prison. He wanted to know how she could continue to believe in God when that same God had allowed her father to die in prison. Before she was able to answer, she was taken back to her cell. But this officer—Lieutenant Rahms—had arranged for Betsie's cell door to be opened just as Corrie was walking past it. It was a brief moment of joy.

June 6, 1944, on the beaches of Normandy, far from Corrie's prison walls, the invasion of Europe by Allied forces had begun. Within a year the terrible war would be over. But it was far from over for Corrie. Around this time, all the inmates in her prison were ordered from their cells and taken by bus to a freight yard. Weeping tears of relief and gratitude, Corrie was finally reunited with Betsie. They had not seen each other in four months. It had been their first separation in fifty-three years.

The prisoners were ordered to board a train, which jerked to a start in the early hours of the morning. Some hours later, they were ordered off in the middle of a wood and told to march for more than a mile until they reached a row of barracks. It was Camp Vught, a concentration camp. This, Corrie realized, would be their new home.

The camp staff assigned work to the prisoners: Betsie was to work sewing prison uniforms; Corrie was to make radios for German flyers. She would do this eleven long hours each day. The foreman in Corrie's barracks factory, Mr. Moorman, had served as headmaster of a Catholic school for boys before the war. One day, as he watched Corrie work on relay switches, he bent down to whisper to her, "'Dear watch lady! Can you not remember for whom you are working? These radios are for their fighter planes!' He reached over to pull a wire loose and twist tubes from their assembly. 'Now solder them back wrong. And not so fast! You're over the day's quota and it's not yet noon.'"[18]

On their lunch breaks the inmates were allowed to wander around the compound freely. Evenings meant conversation with Betsie and the sharing of camp news. Betsie, as usual, spent much time passionately sharing her faith with the women around her and praying with them too.

One day Betsie had disturbing news for Corrie. Through other prisoners, she had discovered the name of the stranger who had betrayed the Ten Booms that fateful day—and who had caused them such pain ever since. The man's name was Jan Vogel. As Corrie later wrote, "I thought of Father's final hours, alone and confused . . . of the Underground work so abruptly halted. . . . And I knew that if Jan Vogel stood in front of me now I could kill him."[19]

But Corrie was astonished at Betsie's reaction to the news. Unlike Corrie, she was completely free of anger. Finally Corrie asked, "Betsie, don't you feel anything about Jan Vogel? Doesn't it bother you?"

"Oh yes, Corrie! Terribly," Betsie replied. "I've felt for him ever since I knew—and pray for him whenever his name comes into my mind. How dreadfully he must be suffering!"[20]

Thinking of her sister's words that night as she tried to sleep, Corrie began to wonder if Betsie, in her gentle way, was reminding her that in God's eyes, she was guilty too. Didn't Jan Vogel and she both stand before an all-seeing God? And according to Jesus's standard in the New Testament, they were both guilty of murder because, Corrie wrote, "I had murdered him with my heart and with my tongue."[21] She prayed that God would forgive her, as she now forgave Jan Vogel, and asked God to bless his family.

While her work on the radios was satisfying, in its way, and the food was a marked improvement over what Corrie and Betsie had been fed in prison, there were still hours of terrible cruelty. For instance, as punishment for some slight violation of the rules by one inmate, all the prisoners were forced to rise at 4:00 a.m. or earlier and stand at attention for an hour or more.

And there was worse to come. One morning in early September 1944, the women were ordered to pack their few possessions. They were marched out of the camp down the same dirt road they had traversed ten weeks earlier, on the night they had arrived. More than one thousand women and many men were forced to board the boxcars of a freight train. Eighty women were jammed in Corrie's car before the door was slammed shut; they screamed, cried, and fainted in an upright position because of the intense press of bodies.

The women found a way to sit, but after many hours in the stationary train, the air inevitably became foul. Finally the train began to move, and for the rest of the day and for the next two days, it traveled in fits and starts as the Germans repaired damaged rail track ahead of them. The miserable passengers fought thirst and hunger and the almost unbearable stench. Then they heard frightening news: they had entered Germany. The women were forced to spend two more days and nights traveling in the filthy boxcar.

On the fourth morning of this hellish trip, the train came to a halt and the door was flung open. Their lips were cracked from thirst, and they were glad at last to relieve their thirst with buckets of water from a nearby lake. Then the women were marched off through a nearby town and into the hills.

Corrie saw a concrete wall surrounding ugly barracks, guard towers, and a smokestack. It was Ravensbrück, the notorious concentration camp for women in northern Germany. This nightmarish place would be Corrie and Betsie's new home. The women spent their first night sleeping fitfully in a field as it rained. The next day all they received to eat was a slice of black bread, some turnip soup, and a boiled potato. And after all they had endured, the women were then forced to stand at attention for the almost inconceivable period of two full days. Then the Germans began to process them, which involved ordering the women to throw all their possessions in a pile, strip naked, and walk before the leering eyes of the Schutzstaffel (S.S.) men on their way to the showers.

Knowing how desperately Betsie needed her vitamins, her sweater, and her Bible, Corrie swiftly cast about for a plan to keep them. She asked a guard where the toilets were. After being directed into the shower room, Corrie spied a pile of prison garb the women were being told to put on and some benches. She quickly wrapped the Bible and the vitamins in the sweater and hid them behind the benches. A few minutes later when she and Betsie returned, naked, to the shower room, Corrie put on a dress and stuffed her bundle down the front. It made quite a bulge, but somehow Corrie knew that God was watching over them.

When she emerged from the shower room, the S.S. men searched each woman thoroughly for contraband—every woman but Corrie. They were searched a second time by female guards. Again each woman was searched except Corrie. What could this be but a miracle? Corrie and Betsie were stunned and tremendously grateful to God. They had no doubt that he had done this.

Betsie and Corrie were assigned to Barracks Eight, where they were told to share a bed already occupied by three women. But because of the outrageous miracle they had just experienced, they carried a new level of faith with them. They also had their precious Bible.

The morning roll call at Ravensbrück was much more brutal than at their previous camp, especially now that the fall weather was growing colder. The women were forced to stand for hours at a time without moving. But worse than this were the terrible sounds coming from the punishment barracks next door, where prisoners screamed as the guards beat them. The smoke from the crematorium reminded them that many among them were dying every day, and as Corrie watched the smoke, she wondered when it would be her turn to die.

As the mindless suffering increased throughout the day, whenever the chance presented itself, the sisters' hidden Bible offered encouragement and hope to the women living in Barracks Eight on dirty mattresses covered in lice.

In October the women were moved to different quarters: a foul-smelling barracks with overflowing toilets and no beds—just wooden structures on which they slept "stacked three high, and wedged side by side and end to end with only an occasional narrow aisle slicing through."[22] The straw atop them was rancid and swarming with fleas.

Corrie was horrified, but Betsie, as usual, responded with patience. She reminded Corrie of the Scripture they had read just that morning. "Rejoice always, pray without ceasing, in everything give thanks; for this is the will of God in Christ Jesus for you" (1 Thess. 5:16–18).

Betsie urged Corrie to join her in doing what the Bible said in that verse, even though—and perhaps especially because—it ran counter to what anyone would have wanted to do. She asked Corrie to join her in thanking God for everything in the barrack—for their Bible, for the fact that they were jammed into a building designed for four hundred people, but which now held fourteen hundred—and even to thank God for the fleas.

This was too much for Corrie. She told her sister, "Betsie, there's no way even God can make me grateful for a flea."[23] But Betsie insisted. She knew that for devout believers in Jesus, doing this was an act of purest obedience to what God said in the Bible. It was, therefore, an act of worship. What harm could come of obeying God and worshiping him? So Corrie relented and begrudgingly thanked God for the fleas.

Every day, after being roused at 4:00 a.m., Corrie, Betsie, and thousands of other prisoners were forced to walk a mile and a half to a factory to work for eleven hours, unloading large metal plates from a boxcar and wheeling them in a handcart elsewhere in the factory. It was exhausting work for women in their fifties, but nevertheless, after returning to the camp and eating a meager dinner, Betsie and Corrie held worship services under the glowing light of a single bulb.

Corrie recalled: "A single meeting might include a recital of the Magnificat in Latin by a group of Roman Catholics, a whispered hymn by some Lutherans, and a sotto voce chant by Eastern Orthodox women. . . . They were little previews of heaven, these evenings beneath the light bulb."[24] The little sermon was translated by the prisoners from Dutch into German, from German into Polish, and into Czech and Russian.

In November the factory work suddenly ceased. Had the factory been bombed? No one knew. The prisoners were now put to back-breaking work leveling the ground inside the camp. One day when Betsie was able to lift only the smallest shovelful of dirt, a guard began to make fun of her. Betsie tried to laugh along with them but only succeeded in infuriating the guard tormenting her. The guard picked up her crop and struck Betsie hard on her neck and chest.

In a blind rage, Corrie grabbed her shovel and went for the guard, but Betsie stopped her before the guard had a chance to see her. As blood began to soak her blouse, she begged her sister to keep working. Seeing Corrie stare angrily at the welt forming on her neck, Betsie said, "Don't look at it, Corrie. Look at Jesus only."[25]

Strangely, when the sisters held their worship services at night, the ever-present guards never came near them or made any effort to stop them. But soon the sisters found out why. One day Betsie asked a supervisor to come into the barracks and answer a question for her. Because of her weakened condition, Betsie had been put to work knitting socks. She had become confused about sock sizes and thought the supervisor could answer the question. But the supervisor wouldn't step through the door. "[N]either would the guards," Betsie explained to Corrie afterward. "And you know why?" Corrie had no idea. "Because of the fleas!" Betsie said.[26] Corrie now remembered how Betsie had pushed her to thank God even for the fleas, and now she suddenly could see God's hand in that prayer too. She was astonished.

God's presence began to reveal itself in another way, and it seemed nothing less than miraculous. Somehow their precious little vitamin bottle never seemed to empty. Corrie put drops on Betsie's bread each day, and Betsie insisted on sharing the drops with many others who were sick. It was impossible to see how much was left in the dark brown glass bottle. But the drops continued to fall, day after day, while fellow prisoners watched in amazement. Then one day a fellow prisoner who worked in the hospital managed to steal a large number of vitamin pills. It was not until that very evening that Corrie discovered that the vitamin bottle was at last empty. These were small mercies, but they revealed the presence of God and were deeply comforting and encouraging.

As winter progressed cold rains began to fall, and the prisoners were forced to stand in puddles during roll call. Inevitably the anemic Betsie weakened further, and one day, with a temperature of 104, she was sent to the hospital. But even there she took the opportunity to tell those around her about Jesus, of his love for them and how he wanted them to enter into a relationship with him.

Unable to stay with her sister, Corrie returned to her barracks, which over the weeks had been transformed by Betsie's loving influence. Instead of bitter cursing and fighting, the inmates now spoke gently to one another. After a friendly inmate told Corrie how she could sneak into the hospital, Corrie went to see Betsie. But because she had been indoors and not forced to work, Betsie was already better.

Three days later Betsie returned to the barracks. No doctor had ever treated her, and she was still feverish. While Betsie was no longer required to work outdoors, she was still forced to endure roll call twice each day outdoors in the December snow. Many of the women, weak and sick, died from this terrible treatment.

During one of these freezing mornings, Betsie and Corrie first envisioned what they would do after the war was over. They were watching in horror as a guard nicknamed "The Snake" sadistically beat a young, feeble-minded girl who had soiled herself while standing for roll call.

"Betsie," Corrie whispered, "what can we do for these people? Afterward, I mean. Can't we make a home for them and care for them?"

"Corrie, I pray every day that we will be allowed to do that! To show them that love is greater!"[27] Not until later did Corrie realize that while she had been thinking of the victims of the Nazis, Betsie was thinking of the Nazis themselves.

When Corrie found out that she was to be sent to work at a munitions factory, she deliberately failed an eye exam so that she might remain behind at Ravensbrück with Betsie. Corrie was assigned to knit socks with her sister. She remembered this time as a deeply joyful one. "In the sanctuary of God's fleas, Betsie and I ministered the word of God to all in the room. We sat beside deathbeds that became doorways of heaven. We watched women who had lost everything grow rich in hope."[28] They interceded for everyone in Ravensbrück.

The sisters continued to dream of the lovely, flower-filled haven they would create after the war for those who had suffered in various ways. It helped keep their minds off the horrifying reality of seeing sick women—women they knew—being helped into trucks and driven to the brick building with the huge smokestack.

How much longer could they endure this frozen hell? How much longer could the war last? One week before Christmas, when the morning siren sounded, Betsie found she could not move her arms or legs. Corrie and another inmate carried her to the hospital only to find a long line snaking out of the building with bodies of those who had died while waiting lying in the snow.

Corrie turned around and carried her sister back to the barracks. There in her filthy bed Betsie lay for the next two days. When she was awake she would mutter about the lovely home they would create for concentration camp victims and about another home in Germany to help those whose minds and hearts had been twisted by Hitler's teachings.

The next day revealed evidence that their prayers for even the most vicious guards were having an effect. As usual, the early morning siren sounded, and following the strict rules of the camp, Corrie and another inmate began to carry Betsie outside to wait in the sleet for the long roll call. But at the barracks door awaited "the Snake." She ordered that Betsie be taken back to her bunk.

Following roll call, Corrie returned to the dormitory to find "the Snake" standing beside her sister. Two orderlies were preparing to lift Betsie onto a stretcher. Corrie wondered if "the Snake" had put aside her fears of being infested by fleas and lice in order to spare Betsie from the rigors of roll call.

Outside, the orderlies took Betsie past the line of inmates waiting for care and into a ward, where she was placed on a cot under a window. All the way to the hospital, Betsie continued to babble about the work they were going to do when they were free, helping others see that "there is no pit so deep that he is not deeper still."[29] And though it made no sense to Corrie, Betsie then said that both she and Corrie would be released from prison by January 1, 1945.

A few hours later Corrie went to visit Betsie. "The Snake" was on duty, and she wrote Corrie a pass. But the hospital nurse refused to allow her into the ward. So she went to the window above Betsie's bed, and the sisters exchanged a few words with each other. Betsie's mind was still on the home they would build.

Later in the day the guards on duty refused to allow Corrie to visit Betsie. The next morning she walked to the window beneath Betsie's bed and looked in. She saw two nurses grasp the edges of a sheet, pick up the human bundle lying on the bed, and carry it away. Her dearest sister was dead.

Betsie's body, like the bodies of other women, was laid out on the floor of a stinking restroom. Fastidious Betsie had always taken such care with her appearance. But when Corrie looked down at her sister, God gave her a loving gift, another astonishing miracle. For no reason that made any sense, naturally speaking, the fifty-nine-year-old Betsie appeared youthful and radiant. As though she had grown young again, the lines of care and grief were erased from her face. This, Corrie believed, was how her sister now looked in heaven.

Three days later, on Christmas Eve, Corrie heard her name called over the loudspeaker. A guard escorted her to an administration barracks. In the street between the barracks, the Germans had erected

Christmas trees, and in a hellish tableau beneath the trees, camp personnel had dumped the bodies of dead women.

At the administration barracks Corrie stood in line behind other women. When her name was called, the officer behind the desk wrote something on a piece of paper, stamped it, and handed it to her. It read: "Certificate of Discharge."

Corrie, like Betsie, was now free. But why? She had no idea. In any event it was a fact: she was soon to be released. Years later she would discover why. The camp officials had made a clerical error. The fact was that all women of her age and older were slated to be killed a week later because of the shortage of food. Miraculously she was spared. Yet in a grotesque irony, after nearly ten months of starvation and myriad forms of torment, the camp officials would not allow Corrie to leave unless she was in good health. A camp doctor diagnosed Corrie with edema of her feet and ankles and ordered her into the hospital.

This final stop on her road to freedom was the worst of all. Trying to sleep her first night at the hospital, Corrie heard mutilated bombing victims screaming in pain. Women fell off their bunks and died where they lay. Nurses behaved viciously.

A few days later Corrie was declared fit enough to leave. It was New Year's Day. What Betsie had predicted in her delirium had come true. Corrie gave her tiny Bible to a Dutch woman, and she herself was given good clothes and food for her journey home. After she was forced to sign a document saying she had been treated well at Ravensbrück, the iron gates opened, and Corrie marched out of the camp in the company of a handful of other women who had been freed. At the little train station the camp guards left them. It was the first time since the day of her arrest that she had been free of their constant presence.

After a long wait she boarded a train and began the long, slow journey to Berlin. Along the way she stared out the window at the ruin of Germany, now just four months away from unconditional surrender to the Allies. After many confusing train changes, she was back in Holland, in the city of Groningen. She could go no farther because Allied bombing had destroyed the rails.

Not knowing where else to go, Corrie limped on painful feet to a nearby hospital. A friendly nurse fed her tea and bread and ran her a hot bath, which soothed her damaged skin. A warm, clean nightgown, clean sheets, soft pillows, gentle hands tucking her in, peace, and privacy—for Corrie, these were a foretaste of heaven itself.

After ten days at the hospital, Corrie was ready to find her way home—to her sister Nollie and brother Willem. The hospital arranged for her to ride on a food truck headed toward Haarlem. And soon, in Willem's house not far from Haarlem and in the tight embrace of her family, she was truly home.

But sad news awaited her. Willem, who had been rearrested and sent to a concentration camp for his resistance work, was dying of spinal tuberculosis. Nor was there any news of his brave son, Kik, who had been deported to Germany; it would be seven years before the family learned that he had died in the Bergen-Belsen concentration camp in 1944.

Many underground members were still hard at work. Corrie longed to go back to Haarlem to visit her surviving sister and to see the Beje. Although several families had lived in the building since the Ten Booms left, it now stood empty. Nollie and her daughters spent many hours cleaning the house for Corrie's arrival.

Inside the Beje a flood of memories of their life in this once-happy home returned to Corrie. Father and Betsie would never return, but others were now running the watch shop for them. As she resumed working behind the counter, she once again reached out to feeble-minded people, bringing them into the Beje. These precious people were among the most helpless of all Haarlem's residents—residents the Nazis had attempted to wipe out.

With the help of others a beautiful Holland home was opened for those who had been damaged by the war: those who had survived concentration camps or spent years hiding in barns and attics. Healing was linked to forgiveness, Corrie wrote. Each had something to forgive, whether it was a neighbor who had turned him in to the Nazi authorities or a vicious camp guard or a brutal soldier.

In mid-May 1945 the Allies marched into Holland, to the unspeakable joy of the Dutch people. Despite the distractions of her work, Corrie was still restless, and she desperately missed her beloved Betsie. But now she remembered Betsie's words: that they must tell others what they had learned.

Thus began more than three decades of travel around the world as a "tramp for the Lord," as Corrie described herself. She told people her story, of God's forgiveness of sins, and of the need for people to forgive those who had harmed them.

Corrie herself was put to the test in 1947 while speaking in a Munich church. At the close of the service, a balding man in a gray overcoat stepped forward to greet her. Corrie froze. She knew this man well; he'd been one of the most vicious guards at Ravensbrück, one who had mocked the women prisoners as they showered. "It came back with a rush," she wrote, "the huge room with its harsh overhead lights; the pathetic pile of dresses and shoes in the center of the floor; the shame of walking naked past this man."

And now he was pushing his hand out to shake hers, and saying:

"A fine message, Fraulein! How good it is to know that, as you say, all our sins are at the bottom of the sea!"

And I, who had spoken so glibly of forgiveness, fumbled in my pocketbook rather than take that hand. He would not remember me, of course—how could he remember one prisoner among those thousands of women?

But I remembered him and the leather crop swinging from his belt. I was face to face with one of my captors, and my blood seemed to freeze.

"You mentioned Ravensbrück in your talk," he was saying. "I was a guard there. . . . But since that time," he went on, "I have become a

Christian. I know that God has forgiven me for the cruel things I did there, but I would like to hear it from your lips as well. Fraulein"— again the hand came out—"will you forgive me?"

And I stood there—I whose sins had again and again to be forgiven—and could not forgive. Betsie had died in that place— could he erase her slow terrible death simply for the asking?

The soldier stood there expectantly, waiting for Corrie to shake his hand. She "wrestled with the most difficult thing I had ever had to do. For I had to do it—I knew that. The message that God forgives has a prior condition: that we forgive those who have injured us."

Standing there before the former S.S. man, Corrie remembered that forgiveness is an act of the will—not an emotion. "Jesus, help me!" she prayed. "I can lift my hand. I can do that much. You supply the feeling."

Corrie thrust out her hand.

And as I did, an incredible thing took place. The current started in my shoulder, raced down my arm, sprang into our joined hands. And then this healing warmth seemed to flood my whole being, bringing tears to my eyes.

"I forgive you, brother!" I cried. "With all my heart."

For a long moment we grasped each other's hands, the former guard and the former prisoner. I had never known God's love so intensely as I did then. But even so, I realized it was not my love. I had tried, and did not have the power. It was the power of the Holy Spirit.[30]

Another man she forgave was Jan Vogel, who had betrayed her and her family that day when he came to the Beje. After the war he was sentenced to death for collaborating with the Nazis, but when she learned of this, Corrie wrote to him, offering her forgiveness and telling him how he could receive Christ.

But her forgiveness aside, Corrie "did not want the Holocaust to be forgotten," wrote historian Lawrence Baron. "Otherwise why would she have written *The Hiding Place* and spent her ministry bearing wit-ness to what happened to the Jews in Holland and to her family for helping them."[31]

On February 28, 1977—thirty-three years to the day of her arrest by the Gestapo—Corrie moved into a small house in Placentia, California. She was eighty-five years old, and after traveling around the world, allowing God to use her to save souls and mend hearts in some sixty countries, it was time to take life a bit slower. For some years Corrie had traveled with a companion, and her current com-panion, Pamela Rosewell, moved in with her. Living near Los Angeles, Corrie believed she could reach even more people, not only through writing books, but also through the making of films aimed at specific audiences. And this is what she did for the next eighteen months.

Soon, though, the first of several severe strokes hit Corrie, leav-ing her mute and later paralyzed. A team of caregivers looked after a deteriorating Corrie for five long, difficult years. On April 15, 1983, her ninety-first birthday, surrounded by birthday bouquets and loving friends, Corrie ten Boom went home to her Lord.

◆ ◆ ◆

The Ten Boom house in Haarlem is now a museum. One can walk up those twisting stairs, over the spot where Corrie hid the radio, to the top floor. There, in Corrie's bedroom, is the hidden closet. The wall has been cut open so that visitors can see into it.

Reading through the many books Corrie wrote, one is struck by her great modesty—her belief that she was not as spiritual as Betsie, nor as patient as her father, nor as smart as her brother, Willem. But her own story is amazing: while in her fifties, this brave maiden lady unhesitatingly became the head of a ring of Dutch underground volunteers entrusted with the lives of her Jewish neighbors. She ful-filled the family commitment to help God's ancient people—work that led to her imprisonment at a concentration camp and to the deaths of her father, sister, brother, and nephew. That work was gratefully recognized by Israel in 1968, when it named Corrie ten Boom a Righteous Gentile and planted a tree in her honor on the Avenue of the Righteous.

SIX

Rosa Parks

1913–2005

I f you have heard of Rosa Parks, you know that this famous woman entered the history books for refusing to give up her seat on a bus. This simple act launched the now-historic yearlong Montgomery bus boycott, which in turn catapulted Martin Luther King Jr. to fame and effectively set in motion the Civil Rights movement. For this reason, Rosa Parks is rightly remembered as the "Mother of the Civil Rights Movement."

But just how did this humble, dignified woman come to be the focal point of this period in American history? And what became of her after that fateful day on that bus? This is her story.

◆ ◆ ◆

R osa McCauley was born in Tuskegee, Alabama, on February 4, 1913, to Leona Edwards McCauley, a schoolteacher, and James McCauley, a carpenter and stonemason.

For Rosa and for most blacks at that time, faith and the church were at the center of life. The church was a welcome, life-filled refuge from the bitterness of that time and place, one known for the lynching and burning of innocent blacks for their alleged crimes against white people. From her earliest years, Rosa loved the words and music of the church. Throughout her life, she attended the African Methodist Episcopal Church.

"Daily devotions played an important part in my childhood," she said. "Every day before supper, and before we went to services on Sundays, my grandmother would read the Bible to me, and my grandfather would pray. . . . I remember finding such comfort and peace while reading the Bible. Its teachings became a way of life and helped me in dealing with my day-to-day problems."[1]

But the Bible had a social mandate in its message too, one that taught Rosa that "people should stand up for rights, just as the children of Israel stood up to the Pharaoh."[2] It was not enough to pray and say that one trusted God. Sometimes trusting God meant taking action too.

During Rosa's earliest years, the economy across the South was in miserable condition, in part because a boll weevil plague had destroyed cotton plants throughout the region. So during Rosa's first years, the McCauleys lived in poverty. When she was two, her family moved to Abbeville, Alabama, to live with Rosa's paternal grandparents and other family. But the conditions were terribly overcrowded, and Leona's mother-in-law was difficult to get along with. As far as Leona was concerned, her husband's unwillingness to look after his family was the worst of it, and before long she packed Rosa off to live with her own parents in Pine Level, Alabama. Rosa saw almost nothing of her father after that.

She and her mother began attending the church at Mount Zion African Methodist Episcopal Church where her uncle preached. Life in Pine Level was easier. For one thing, there was plenty of food. On special occasions, Rosa remembered that the family feasted on ham with red-eye gravy, catfish, or rabbit, with ample sides of turnip greens, peas, and onions and a dessert of sweet potato pie.

Rosa's grandfather Edwards had been born during slavery times, and he taught her about the family history. He also taught her a lesson in self-protection against hostile whites. In 1919, when she was six, the long-dormant Ku Klux Klan became active again. "The Ku Klux Klan was riding through the black community, burning churches, beating up people, killing people," Rosa recalled. "By the time I was six, I was old enough to realize that we were not actually free."[3]

To protect his family, Grandfather Edwards told the children to wear their clothes to bed "so we would be ready to run if we had to," Rosa wrote. Nor was his double-barreled shotgun ever far from hand. Rosa vividly remembered her grandfather saying, "I don't know how long I would last if they came breaking in here, but I'm getting the first one who comes through the door." Rosa tried to stay awake as long as she could each night, hoping not to miss seeing her grandfather shoot an intruder. Mercifully no one ever attacked the family. But experiences like these, according to historian Douglas Brinkley, taught Rosa that "it wasn't enough to just 'turn a cheek' in Christian submission when one's very life was at stake."[4]

Rosa learned other hard lessons in oppression. She worked barefoot picking cotton for Moses Hudson, a local planter, for fifty cents a day, from sunup to sundown. The hot sand burned the children's feet, and when their feet were too blistered to stand on, they were made to pick cotton on their knees. If they accidentally dripped blood on the cotton, they were punished.

But there were good times too. Rosa enjoyed playing games with her little brother, Sylvester, and their friends. She was grateful she could earn some extra money by selling eggs to the neighbors. She loved wandering through Alabama's piney woods, and she even enjoyed attending school.

But racism was ever present in her life. Rosa remembered enduring insults from white children as she walked to school; they threw rocks at her and called her "nigger." But her faith sustained her, and early on she would recite specific Bible verses to herself, so that she could face her persecutors with peace and courage. Psalm 23 was one of her favorites, as was Psalm 27, whose first lines read: "The LORD is my light and my salvation; whom shall I fear? The LORD is the strength of my life; of whom shall I be afraid?"

When Rosa was eleven, she began attending the Montgomery Industrial School for Girls, also called Miss White's School. All the teachers in the school were white, as was Miss White herself, and all three hundred students were black. Students were taught cooking, sewing, housekeeping, and how to care for the sick at home, lessons that—at a time when few blacks were permitted access to hospitals— would be useful to Rosa in later years. Each day included Bible reading and prayer. But dancing, going to the movies, and wearing makeup were forbidden.

Rosa recalled that what she learned best at Miss White's School "was that I was a person with dignity and self-respect and I should not set my sights lower than anybody just because I was black. We were taught to be ambitious and to believe that we could do what we wanted in life."[5] Tragically the school was burned down by hostile whites and then closed for good when Rosa was fifteen. But she never forgot Miss White, whose dedicated efforts on behalf of her charges played a role in putting Rosa on the path to civil rights activism.

Rosa attended Booker T. Washington Junior High and completed tenth and eleventh grades at the laboratory school of the Alabama State Teachers College for Negroes. She dreamed of becoming a teacher like her mother, but when her grandmother grew ill, Rosa had to cut her education short so that she could care for her. After her grandmother's death, sixteen-year-old Rosa went to work at a textile factory, sewing men's shirts. Then her mother fell ill, and she had to leave the factory to care for her. Rosa wasn't happy about leaving either her school or the factory, but she endured these things without complaint. Every Sunday, she attended the St. Paul AME Church, which she loved.

In 1931, when she was eighteen, Rosa met her future husband, Raymond Parks, a twenty-eight-year-old barber and church sexton. He was also a charter member of the Montgomery chapter of the National Association for the Advanced of Colored People (NAACP). At first, Rosa was not eager to pursue the relationship, but Raymond, who was smitten with Rosa, was persistent. Eventually she agreed to go for a ride in his sporty red Nash. As the couple got to know each other, Rosa found herself impressed "by the fact that [Raymond] didn't seem to have that meek attitude—what we called an 'Uncle Tom' attitude— toward white people. I thought he was a very nice man, an interesting man who talked very intelligently."[6]

Under Raymond's tutelage, Rosa began to pay more attention to civil rights issues, especially the 1931 case of the Scottsboro Boys, nine black teenagers who had been accused of raping two white prostitutes. Eight of them were convicted and sentenced to death. But in a desperate effort to keep them from being executed, Raymond worked to raise money to pay for legal help. Because their work was so dangerous— police had actually murdered members of their group—Raymond refused to allow Rosa to become involved. In the end four of the young men went free, while the remaining five were given long prison terms.

Rosa could not help admiring Raymond's courage. They were married in December 1932. Raymond encouraged his wife to go back to school and earn her high school diploma, which she did when she was twenty years old, becoming one of the few blacks in Montgomery to do so. But it was still the 1930s, and Rosa's high school diploma didn't impress white Southern employers. So she earned money by sewing and working at a hospital. She later obtained a job at Maxwell Army Air Force base.

Traveling to and from the base was a daily exercise in humiliation. On the trolley at the base, Rosa could sit anywhere she chose, because President Franklin Roosevelt had prohibited segregation on military bases. If "negroes," as they were then called, could put on the uniform of the United States and risk their lives for their country, surely they were equal to the whites who were doing the same thing and shouldn't have to sit in a segregated area. But when Rosa stepped off the base trolley and climbed onto a city bus, the rules were different: she had to sit in the back.

Nor was this the only insult she and millions of other black Americans were forced to endure. In the 1930s and 1940s, blacks lived in a world of separate drinking fountains, separate restrooms, and separate elevators. Rosa, offended by this, avoided using these facilities in order to preserve her dignity, taking the stairs rather than riding the "colored" elevator and going home rather than using the "colored" restrooms.

After his work in the Scottsboro case was over, Raymond turned his attention to the issue of voting rights. At that time in Alabama, if you were black, it was nearly impossible to register to vote. Raymond and Rosa began holding meetings in their home at night to discuss strategies. But they made little progress until E. D. Nixon, a railroad porter and president of the Montgomery Branch of the NAACP, joined them. He was also president of the local branch of the Brotherhood of Sleeping Car Porters, a black railroad workers' union. Nixon worked with Arthur Madison, a black lawyer who practiced in New York. Madison explained how blacks should go about attempting to register, explaining to them that they would be asked to take a literacy test.

In 1943 Rosa decided to register to vote. Simply finding out what time city hall opened its doors was difficult, as city workers, in an effort to keep black citizens from registering, constantly changed the times and days that people could register. Finally, on her day off, Rosa went to city hall to take the test. Whites were given their certificates immediately if they passed the test, but black citizens had to wait for their certificates to arrive in the mail. Rosa never received hers. She took the test a second time and was again told she hadn't passed.

Undeterred, Rosa went back a third time, took the test, and made copies of all her answers, intending to sue the voter-registration board if it once again denied her the right to vote. This time her certificate arrived. But another hurdle stood before her: she had to pay

the accumulated poll tax from the year she had turned twenty-one—
something white voters did not have to do. The amount for Rosa was
$16.50, no small amount of money in the 1940s. Still, she was able to
vote for governor for the first time, and she voted for Jim Folsom.

◆ ◆ ◆

Even before Rosa's birth, boycotts of segregated streetcars took
place throughout the South as a result of the infamous 1896 *Plessy
v. Ferguson* Supreme Court decision, which upheld state "separate
but equal" laws affecting public facilities. These boycotts have largely
been forgotten, but between 1900 and 1910, boycotts of segregated
streetcars took place in no fewer than twenty-seven cities in the Deep
South. One massive protest took place in Montgomery, where, after
five weeks, the company that operated the trolleys saw its profits drop
by 25 percent. The company had no choice but to give in and integrate
its streetcars.

The integration was short-lived, however. Rosa was aware of this
early boycott. "I thought about it sometimes when the segregated
trolley passed by. It saddened me to think how we had taken one foot
forward and two steps back,"[7] she recalled.

In the 1940s, bus drivers carried guns and had "police power" to
rearrange the seating on the bus any way they chose. Very few people are
aware of the fact that, twelve years before Rosa Parks made her historic
1955 stand against the segregated bus rule, she had another run-in with
bus driver James F. Blake over an issue of segregation. Blake forced her
off his bus because she had refused to obey his demand that she pay the
fare at the front door and then get off the bus and reenter through the
back door. This was common treatment for black riders. Rosa decided to
buck this custom. "One day in the winter of 1943," she wrote,

> the bus came along, and the back was crowded with black people.
> They were even standing on the steps leading up from the back door.

But up front there were vacant seats. . . . So I got on at the front and went through this little bunch of folks standing in the back, and I looked toward the front and saw the driver standing there and looking at me. He told me to get off the bus and go to the back door and get on. I told him I was already on the bus and didn't see the need of getting off and getting back on when people were standing in the stepwell, and how was I going to squeeze on anyway?

So he told me if I couldn't go through the back door that I would have to get off the bus. . . . I stood where I was.

He looked like he was ready to hit me. I said, "I know one thing. You better not hit me." He didn't strike me. I got off.[8]

The man had been so vile that Rosa refused to ever again board any bus he was driving, even if it meant walking home in the rain. Neither she nor the driver in their wildest dreams could have imagined that twelve years later, they would again square off against each other in a historic showdown that would change the entire country forever.

Thanks to her husband's influence, Rosa was becoming more and more active in civil rights efforts. One day in 1943 she showed up at a local meeting of the NAACP when an election of officers was taking place. Rosa was the only woman there, and when she was asked to become secretary, she was too shy to refuse. Her job—unpaid—was to take the minutes of meetings, write articles, send letters and membership payments to the NAACP's national offices, answer the telephone, and deal with press releases.

Among Rosa's most important duties was keeping track of discrimination cases and violent attacks on blacks. This was work that might have embittered a lesser person. For instance, white women who accused blacks of rape received swift attention. But when a black woman was gang-raped by white men, no charges were brought—even in the case of Mrs. Recy Taylor, in which one of the rapists confessed and implicated the other five attackers. Moreover, witnesses to white-on-black violence were often too frightened to testify. Rosa recalled that the NAACP "didn't have too many successes in getting justice. It was more a matter of trying to challenge the powers that be, and to let it be known that we did not wish to continue being second-class citizens."[9]

The violence became even worse after the Second World War, in which many African Americans had nobly fought. Having served their country, they believed they deserved equal treatment. Among them was Rosa's brother, Sylvester, who became so frustrated by his treatment at the hands of racist whites in Alabama that he moved north to Detroit, Michigan.

By the late 1940s Rosa was both secretary of the Senior Branch of the Montgomery NAACP and an adviser to its Youth Council, which engaged in such tactics as checking out books from the city's library for whites instead of the poorly equipped library for blacks. Rosa also performed volunteer work at the union offices of E. D. Nixon. In 1954 Nixon introduced Rosa to someone who would become very important in her life: a white woman named Virginia Durr, who, along with her husband, was active in civil rights work. Durr promptly hired Rosa to do some sewing for her and invited her to take part in an integrated prayer group, which ended abruptly when the husbands of the white women found out about it.

The year 1954 offered a ray of hope for black Americans when the Supreme Court outlawed segregation in schools in *Brown v. the Board of Education*. "You can't imagine the rejoicing among black people, and some white people, when the Supreme Court decision came down in May 1954," Rosa wrote. "The Court had said that separate education could not be equal, and many of us saw how the same idea applied to other things, like public transportation."[10]

Rosa learned more political tactics when, in the summer of 1955, Durr suggested she attend a workshop at the Highlander Folk School in Tennessee, titled "Racial Desegregation: Implementing the Supreme

Court Decision." The school was run by whites, but it was here that Rosa not only attended workshops on desegregation, but also encountered great generosity by supportive whites, who did everything from picking her up at the bus stop to cooking her breakfast. After ten enjoyable days, it was back to segregated Montgomery and her job as an assistant tailor at the Montgomery Fair department store.

◆ ◆ ◆

Since whites were typically able to afford cars while blacks were not, far more black citizens rode Montgomery's buses than did whites. This made it all the more galling that black riders were forced to sit in the back of the bus or relinquish their seats when a white person got on. Black leaders began to attempt small changes in how blacks were treated on public transportation—such as getting buses to stop at every corner in black neighborhoods as they did in white ones. But for the most part city leaders simply paid no attention.

Around this time Rosa and others began to think about a boycott. Since blacks comprised more than 66 percent of the Montgomery bus ridership, a boycott would make quite an impact. But for a boycott to work, huge numbers of black riders would have to agree to find other ways to get to work. This was asking a lot of people who were already strapped with enough things to think about and do during a busy day.

The Montgomery NAACP also considered filing suit against the city to enforce desegregation on public transportation. For this they needed not only a strong case, but the right plaintiff. They decided it needed to be a woman, because they knew that a female would garner more sympathy than a man. And they agreed that the woman had to be someone of high moral character, so she could not be attacked for anything other than having refused to sacrifice her seat on a bus.

One young woman seemed a possibility: Claudette Colvin, whom police had arrested when she refused to give up her seat to a white rider. But fifteen-year-old Claudette was pregnant—and unmarried.

"They'd call her a bad girl, and her case wouldn't have a chance," Rosa recalled.[11] The answer to the local NAACP leaders' problem was staring them right in the face. They just didn't know it, and neither did the demure forty-two-year-old seamstress.

On the cold evening of December 1, 1955, the woman who had been taught from childhood to love her enemies, but not take any guff from them, put away her work and walked out of Montgomery Fair department store at five o'clock. Store windows proclaimed the coming holiday with toy trains, bright sweaters, and a huge Christmas tree covered with blinking electric lights. Rosa left early that evening because she had a meeting in another town, but even so, she was tired from the long hours sewing, ironing, and steampressing.

Rosa walked to the bus stop one block away. Because it was just after five, a huge crowd of people was congregated there, so Rosa decided not to get on that bus. She thought she would be better off catching the next one. She killed some time doing a little Christmas shopping at Lee's Cut-Rate Drugstore. Then back to the bus stop she went, wondering what her mother planned to cook for their dinner and thinking about that evening's NAACP Youth Council meeting.

With her mind preoccupied Rosa did not notice whose bus she was stepping onto, but when the bus driver swiveled around to stare at Rosa, she realized to her shock and dismay that it was James F. Blake, the very driver who had put her off the bus twelve years before. This time, however, the tired seamstress and the bigoted bus driver were about to make history.

Finding a vacant seat in the middle section of the bus, behind the sign reading "colored," Rosa tiredly sat down. Three other blacks were also seated in that row. In front of Rosa were several "whites only" seats.

Blake stepped on the gas, and the bus trundled on down the street. After two more stops, white passengers filled most of the seats in the front section. At the third stop, in front of the Empire Theater, the last "whites only" seats were occupied, and one white man was left standing.

Blake swiveled around and stared at Rosa. "Let me have those front seats," he ordered.

According to the law, no black person could sit in the same row as a white person—meaning all four blacks in the row Rosa occupied would have to move to accommodate one white man. Silence met the driver's command. Nobody moved. Angered, Blake tried again. "Y'all better make it light on yourselves and let me have those seats," he warned.[12]

The two women sitting across the aisle from Rosa and the man sitting next to her got up and moved to the back of the bus. But Rosa was not about to move. Instead, she simply slid over to the window seat and stared out at the Empire Theater marquee, which announced that week's film: *A Man Alone*, starring Ray Milland, a western about a man who faces down a village for a crime he did not commit.

Blake saw that one of the four had ignored his demand, and he was not going to let one small black woman make a fool of him. He got out of his seat and began walking down the aisle toward Rosa.

"I thought back to the time when I used to sit up all night and didn't sleep, and my grandfather would have his gun right by the fireplace, or if he had his one-horse wagon going anywhere, he always had his gun in the back of the wagon," Rosa said. "People always say that I didn't give up my seat because I was tired, but that isn't true. I was not tired physically, or no more tired than I usually was at the end of a working day. . . . No, the only tired I was, was tired of giving in."[13]

Rosa also thought of Dr. Martin Luther King Jr.'s words: "Some of us must bear the burden of trying to save the soul of America."[14]

Blake was now standing over Rosa. "Are you going to stand up?" he asked, urgently.

Rosa looked him straight in the eye and with great dignity responded, "No."

"Well, I'm going to have to have you arrested."

"You may do that,"[15] Rosa replied.

Blake radioed to his supervisor, who, after asking Blake if he had warned Rosa, told him to go ahead and put her off the bus. Waiting for the police to arrive, many nervous passengers got off the bus not wanting to be involved in whatever was going to happen next. Rosa was nervous herself. She wasn't thinking about possibly becoming the NAACP test case; she was wondering if the police would beat her up as well as arrest her.

Two Montgomery police officers, D. W. Mixon and F. B. Day, arrived, and Blake told them what had happened. They then boarded the bus and approached Rosa. "Why," Officer Day asked her, "did you refuse to stand up when the driver spoke to you?"

Rosa stared back at him. "Why do you all push us around?" she said.

"I don't know," Day replied, "but the law is the law, and you're under arrest."[16]

The two officers escorted Rosa off the yellow-olive bus and into their squad car. In his book, *Rosa Parks: A Life*, historian Douglas Brinkley wrote, "They did not handcuff Parks or mistreat her in any way. In fact, Parks saw them as two tired beat cops with no desire to waste their time and effort writing up reports for minor offenses."[17]

At city hall, a thirsty Rosa asked to get a drink of water at a nearby fountain. Officer Day told her to go ahead and take a drink, but Officer Mixon intervened, shouting, "You can't drink no water. It's for whites only. You have to wait till you get to the jail."[18]

"That made me angry," Rosa later wrote, and the incident made her think of the Roman soldiers who had given the thirsty Christ vinegar to drink as he hung on the cross.[19] She asked if she could use the telephone and was told she could not. More racism, she thought.

After Rosa filled out the required forms, she was taken back out to the police squad car for the trip to the city jail. By now she was chuckling to herself. As Brinkley wrote, "Who would have thought that little Rosa McCauley—whose friends teased her for being such a Goody Two-shoes in her dainty white gloves—would ever become a convicted criminal, much less a subversive worthy of police apprehension, in the eyes of the state of Alabama?"[20]

At the jail Rosa was fingerprinted and photographed. Again she asked for a drink of water and was again refused. She was then escorted upstairs to a second-floor cell. They locked her in and left. Returning moments later the female guard sympathetically asked Rosa if she would prefer sharing a cell with two other black women instead of being by herself. Rosa didn't really care one way or another, but she agreed to move. Once again she asked if she could make a telephone call to let her husband know where she was. The guard said she would check.

A while later, Rosa was allowed to call home. "I'm in jail. See if Parks will come down here and get me out," she told her mother.

"Did they beat you?" Rosa's mother asked.

"No, I wasn't beaten, but I am in jail."[21]

Overhearing his mother-in-law's side of the conversation, a horrified Raymond Parks grabbed the phone, demanding to know if his wife had been harmed. No, she replied, the police had not harmed her or even verbally abused her. Parks told her he would be at the station in a few minutes. While she waited, one of her cell mates gave her a cup of water.

Meanwhile, news of Rosa's arrest spread rapidly through the black community. E. D. Nixon attempted to discover what Rosa was being charged with and called attorney Clifford Durr, the husband of Rosa's friend Virginia. Durr was able to find out both the charges and the amount of the bail, while Raymond Parks called a white friend of his whom he knew would be able to provide the bail money.

That evening the jail matron told Rosa she was free to go. On her way out she spotted Virginia Durr, who hugged her. Clifford Durr and Nixon were there too. Rosa was given a trial date four days later. She remembered that they had left without saying much to each other. But the experience of being in jail had deeply upset Rosa. Her husband arrived in a borrowed car and took Rosa home. As her family and friends comforted her that evening, Rosa vowed never again to ride a segregated bus. But suddenly, for the very first time, something occurred to all of them. Rosa herself might make the perfect plaintiff in a test case of segregation law. She seemed tailor-made for the role. She was a churchgoing woman, decidedly dignified and decent. Nobody could say she had done anything to deserve such wretched treatment—except to be born of black parents.

Meanwhile black leaders realized this was the time to launch a boycott of the city buses. It would begin the day Rosa's trial was to take place. They printed thirty-five thousand handbills announcing the boycott during the night and dropped them off at Montgomery's black schools. "Another Negro woman has been arrested and thrown in jail because she refused to get up out of her seat on the bus for a white person to sit down," the handbill announced. "We are . . . asking every Negro to stay off the buses Monday in protest of the arrest and trial."[22]

Black ministers also got involved in the boycott effort, calling a meeting at Dexter Avenue Baptist Church on the evening after Rosa's arrest. Nixon contacted the press, hoping for front-page coverage.

At the Dexter Avenue Baptist Church meeting, Rosa described what had taken place on the bus. Most of the ministers agreed to talk about the boycott during their Sunday sermons. A local newspaper, the *Montgomery Advertiser*, reproduced the handbill on page one. But would that be enough? Getting the word out far and wide was crucial, because unless enough black citizens stayed off the buses the following day, the boycott simply wouldn't make the necessary impact.

Montgomery had eighteen black-owned cab companies, and to help people who had a long bus ride to work, they all agreed to pick up black passengers at the city's bus stops and to charge only the amount of bus fare.

When Monday arrived, vast numbers of Montgomery's black citizens stayed off the buses. They took cabs, they walked, and they carpooled. Some of them even rode mules and buggies. As for the buses, they rode around the city empty, or nearly empty, all day. The boycott was a tremendous success.

That day Rosa arrived at the courthouse dressed in a neat black dress. She was surrounded by huge crowds of people who had come to support her. Spotting Rosa, a young girl shouted joyfully, "Oh, she's so sweet. They've messed with the wrong one now."[23]

Blake, the bus driver, testified that Rosa had refused to move when he told her to, and a white woman testified, untruthfully, that Rosa had refused to take a vacant seat in the back of the bus. Rosa's attorneys, Charles Langford and Fred Gray, entered Rosa's "not guilty" plea. But they were not interested in winning this case.

"They did not intend to try to defend me against the charges," Rosa recalled. "The point of making mine a test case was to allow me to be found guilty and then to appeal the conviction to a higher court. Only in higher courts could the segregation laws actually be changed."[24]

To no one's surprise, Rosa was found guilty and ordered to pay a ten-dollar fine, plus four dollars in court costs.

That evening another meeting was held at Holt Street Baptist Church. The Reverend Ralph Abernathy, along with several other ministers, decided to form the Montgomery Improvement Association (MIA). The association elected as its first president the brilliant twenty-five-year-old minister Martin Luther King Jr.

By now, support for Rosa's brave act had swelled. The church was packed while hundreds more stood outside. The big question was, should they continue the boycott? If so, for how long? How long would white Montgomery put up with a boycott before retaliating?

King, who had received his doctorate six months earlier, rose and gave an extemporaneous speech, although the cadences and words were as lapidary as anything polished through several drafts:

There comes a time that people get tired . . . tired of being segregated and humiliated, tired of being kicked about by the brutal feet of oppression. . . . But we come here tonight to be saved from that patience that makes us patient with anything less than freedom and justice. . . . One of the great glories of democracy is the right to protest for right. . . . [I]f you will protest courageously and yet with dignity and Christian love, when the history books are written in future generations the historians will pause and say, "There lived a great people—a black people—who injected new meaning and dignity into the veins of civilization."[25]

Abernathy asked the assembly to vote by standing up regarding whether to continue the boycott until needed changes were made in public transportation. As Rosa wrote, "Every single person in that church was standing, and outside the crowd was cheering 'Yes!'"[26]

The next day King and other leaders presented their demands to the city commissioners and bus company representatives: more courteous treatment, hiring black drivers for black neighborhoods, and a first-come, first-served seating rule, but with blacks still riding at the back of the bus. But the commissioners and bus company would not accept any of these terms; they refused to budge. The boycott would continue.

Quite incredibly the black community was able to continue the boycott for 381 days. In all that time, no blacks in Montgomery took the buses, ever. It's difficult to imagine how they did it, but the boycott continued, despite harassment from white police officers.

Rosa's refusal to leave her seat had spawned a movement that began to get national attention. Citizens from all over America learned of the boycott and heard about all the people who had been fired from their jobs for supporting the boycott. Rosa herself was discharged from her department store job, but this freed her up to spend more time working for the MIA. Sympathizers in other states sent shoes and clothing to be distributed to people who needed them because they were no longer working—or because they were wearing out shoe leather walking long distances to and from work each day. Rosa was invited to speak publicly about her arrest and took in sewing to help pay the bills.

The white police of Montgomery bore down hard to counteract the boycott. They arrested black cab drivers for charging bus fare instead of the higher cab fare. Volunteer drivers immediately replaced them, however, and took people to work in station wagons purchased by black churches. In fact, Rosa became a dispatcher for this irregular cab service. In time thirty-four private cars and church-owned station wagons were making the rounds, taking some thirty thousand blacks to work each day. Amusingly, many white women began driving their black maids to and from their homes because they couldn't get along without them. Despite anonymous threats and an appeal from the mayor, white women continued to do this.

The boycott led to more serious repercussions—and whites became angrier and angrier, until violence broke out. Both the homes of King and Nixon were bombed, but fortunately, no one was harmed.

Meanwhile Rosa's appeal of her guilty verdict was thrown out on a technicality. But in February 1956 lawyer Fred Gray filed suit in a U.S. district court on behalf of five black women who had been treated badly on city buses. The hope was now to have all segregation on buses outlawed altogether.

The next attack on the boycott was unexpected and ludicrous. White attorneys located an old law on the books that actually outlawed boycotts. A grand jury immediately sprang into action, handing down eighty-nine indictments against King, more than twenty other ministers, leaders of the MIA, and other citizens. "I was re-indicted,"[27] Rosa recalled.

But the whole world was following every detail. The *New York Times* ran a picture of Rosa being fingerprinted on its front page. After the MIA paid their bail, everyone who had been arrested went home.

The only person who was actually put on trial was King. He was found guilty and was given the choice of paying a five-hundred-dollar fine or spending a year in prison doing hard labor. He decided to stay in jail and spent two weeks there before his conviction was overturned on appeal.

But these indictments and King's trial only increased the determination of Montgomery blacks to keep the boycott going. Meanwhile

Rosa continued to speak wherever she could. She was invited to speak even in New York and San Francisco and traveled there to spread the word about what was happening in Montgomery.

In June, Montgomery's black citizens were delighted when a federal district court ruled in their favor in *Browder v. Gale*. The city appealed the decision to the Supreme Court, so the boycott continued, despite baroque new efforts by whites to interfere with it—such as preventing the church-owned station wagons from getting insurance. It took the creative intervention of King to get Lloyd's of London to issue a policy that white Alabamans couldn't get canceled.

The city made one last try at breaking the boycott by claiming that those waiting for private transportation on street corners were a public nuisance. Why they hadn't been considered a public nuisance while waiting for the buses prior to the boycott was never explained. The mayor even managed to get a judge to agree with this, but in the end it was a Pyrrhic victory, because on that very same day—November 13, 1956—the U.S. Supreme Court ruled that it was unconstitutional to segregate riders on city buses. Montgomery blacks exploded with joy when they learned of it, but they still continued to stay off the buses until the city had received the court's official written order. That would take weeks. But when it finally arrived on December 20, the black citizens of Montgomery, Alabama, finally began riding the buses again.

It was a heroic 381-day effort, one that had demanded tremendous sacrifices. But as a result, they had changed the law and had begun a movement that would change America forever.

When the boycott was over, the press asked Rosa to get on a bus and sit in the front seat so they could take pictures of her, which she did. A white male reporter proudly sat behind her to make the point that the days of blacks going to the back of the bus were over.

The transition to unsegregated city buses did not go entirely smoothly. Segregation had been a part of the lives of the people of Montgomery for so long that some whites thought ending it would destroy the very order of things, would wreak havoc with everything they knew and held dear. Shots were fired at some buses, in one case hitting a pregnant woman in the legs. Shots were also fired through King's front door. One day some whites attacked a black teenager as she exited her bus. City leaders pushed back by increasing segregation in other areas of Montgomery life. Death threats against Rosa became so frequent and so frightening that she and Raymond move to Detroit in 1957, where Rosa's brother lived.

But history was moving decidedly against segregation across the country, in large part because of what Rosa had spawned in Montgomery. In other Southern cities civil rights activists, who had observed what happened in Montgomery, began their own bus boycotts.

◆ ◆ ◆

After moving to a Detroit apartment with her husband and mother, Rosa continued speaking out about her experiences. During a visit to Boston, she was introduced to the president of the Hampton Institute, a black institution of higher learning in Hampton, Virginia. He offered Rosa a job as a hostess at a campus residence and guest-house. Her job would entail managing the off-campus guests, as well as the faculty and staff who lived there. Rosa accepted the job and moved to Virginia. She enjoyed the work but missed her husband and mother, who had to remain behind in Detroit. Eventually she resigned and moved back to Detroit. She began working as a seamstress again and kept up her friendship with King, who by now had formed the Southern Christian Leadership Conference. Rosa attended SCLC conventions and put in an appearance whenever a march or demonstration took place in a Southern city.

In 1963 Rosa took part in the historic March on Washington, held to pressure the federal government to pass federal civil rights laws. "The civil-rights movement was having a big effect," Rosa recalled. "It didn't change the hearts and minds of many white Southerners, but it did make a difference to the politicians in Washington, D.C."[28]

The passage of the 1964 Civil Rights Act was a tremendous victory. It guaranteed African Americans the right to vote and outlawed segregation in all public accommodations. This law "did not solve all our problems," Rosa said. "But it gave black people some protection, and some way to get redress for unfair treatment."[29]

In Selma, Alabama, a town that still made it difficult for blacks to vote, the leaders of the SCLC staged a large demonstration. Many deliberately got themselves arrested with the idea of packing the jails. Sheriff Jim Clark and his men, angered by the demonstration, "surrounded a group of about 150 children who were demonstrating downtown. They herded them out of town like cattle, making them trot along the country roads and using electric cattle prods to force them to keep up the pace,"[30] Rosa recalled.

But this backfired dramatically. Out-of-town television reporters caught the scene on camera. As a result the entire country finally woke up to just how badly whites were treating blacks in the South. Support for their cause increased greatly, and when King announced a fifty-mile march from Selma to Montgomery, people came from all over the country to take part, black and white alike. Rosa marched in front with King and his wife, Ralph Abernathy, and other leaders. Three thousand others marched and sang behind them. Every evening at their campsite the world-famous singer Harry Belafonte performed for them.

Once the marchers arrived at Montgomery, the state capital, many whites jeered at them. One white female marcher was murdered by the Klan. Viola Liuzzo had traveled to Alabama from Detroit to take part in the march. Her crime? She had been riding in a car with a black man.

In 1965 President Lyndon Johnson signed the Voting Rights Act—another consequence of peaceful protests. This important law, according to Rosa, meant that "blacks who were denied the chance to register to vote by local officials could get registered by federal examiners."[31] She became convinced of the efficacy of large, nonviolent demonstrations and boycotts, even though she continued to believe that in some situations, as with self-defense, violence was sometimes necessary.

When Rosa was fifty-one, black attorney John Conyers ran for Congress from Michigan's First Congressional District. He asked Rosa to endorse him. He won the seat, and following his victory, she went to work for him in his Detroit office in 1965 as a receptionist and secretary. She would stay for twenty-three years.

Rosa was at home with her mother when she heard over the radio of the shooting of her old friend, Dr. Martin Luther King Jr. on April 4, 1968. She and her mother wept together, and Rosa attended her friend's funeral in Atlanta. But she did not take a bus there; instead she flew in Harry Belafonte's private plane as a guest of honor. At the King home Rosa met Robert Kennedy, the brother of President John F. Kennedy, who had been assassinated five years earlier. Rosa was saddened again when, just two months later, Robert Kennedy himself was cut down by an assassin's bullet.

During the 1970s Rosa began losing the people she loved most. Both she and her husband had been hospitalized for stomach ulcers, but now her beloved husband developed a more serious disease: throat cancer. He died in 1977 at the age of seventy-four. They had been married nearly forty-five years. Rosa's brother Sylvester also died of cancer just three months later. Then in 1979 her ninety-one-year-old mother died of cancer too.

Wishing to both memorialize her husband and help young people, Rosa founded the Rosa and Raymond Parks Institute for Self Development in 1987, which attempted to inspire Detroit young people to "pursue their education and create a promising future for themselves."[32] She also established the Rosa L. Parks Scholarship Foundation, donating her speaking fees to fund college scholarships for promising young African Americans.

This generous habit of donating her speaker's fees would cause problems later on. Rosa lived on her salary from Conyers's office, along with her husband's pension. But as Rosa began suffering from health problems, medical bills piled up, while her income fell from so much time off from her job. The resulting financial squeeze forced Rosa to accept contributions from churches.

Rosa published her autobiography, *My Story*, in 1992, and a second book, *Quiet Strength*, three years later. This second book reveals, in ways other biographies do not, how great a role Rosa's faith in God played throughout her long life and through her struggles. "As a child I learned from the Bible to trust in God and not be afraid,"[33] Rosa wrote. And "I felt the Lord would give me the strength to endure whatever I had to face. God did away with all my fear."[34]

She also wrote that during the early years of the civil rights movement, "one thing we used to keep us going was the moving words of certain hymns, many of which had been passed down from the slave days. . . . Singing gave us the feeling that—with God's help—we could overcome whatever we were facing."[35]

When she faced arrest for refusing to give up her bus seat to a white man and knew they might brutally beat her, "I knew that He was with me, and only He could get me through the next step."[36]

In 1994 Rosa wrote a third book, *Dear Mrs. Parks: A Dialogue with Today's Youth*, which reproduced some of the many letters children sent to her and the loving advice Rosa offered to them. While Rosa became weary of being asked repeatedly about a single day in her life and disliked violations of her privacy, she knew she had become a symbol, and she was grateful for the chance to travel, help a new generation of civil rights activists, and meet the likes of Eleanor Roosevelt and President Bill Clinton.

Rosa came to be called the "Mother of the Civil Rights Movement." As this iconic woman entered her seventies and eighties, towns, cities, and organizations across America heaped honors on her. Among the most important was changing the name of Cleveland Avenue in Montgomery, Alabama, to Rosa Parks Boulevard. Rosa had been riding a bus on that very avenue when she was arrested many years before. And the bus on which she made history is now in the Henry Ford Museum.

In 1990 Rosa was invited to be part of the welcoming committee for Nelson Mandela's arrival in Detroit. Recognizing her, Mandela delightedly began chanting Rosa's name and hugged her. In 1994 she traveled to Stockholm, Sweden, to accept the Rosa Parks Peace Prize. In 1996 President Clinton awarded her the Presidential Medal of Freedom; in 1999 the U.S. Congress awarded Rosa the Congressional Gold Medal. *Time* magazine named Rosa "one of the twenty most influential and iconic figures of the twentieth century."

Troy University in Montgomery, Alabama—the city where she was arrested many years before—dedicated the Rosa Parks Library and Museum in 2000. Children performed plays memorializing Rosa's refusal to give up her seat on the bus.

In 1994, when Rosa was eighty-one years old, she made headlines again when a young black man named Joseph Skipper broke into her Detroit home, demanded money, and repeatedly struck her in the face. Rosa was rushed to a hospital and treated for severe bruising. But while the nation's editorial writers expressed fury with Skipper for assaulting a national treasure, Rosa noted that he was very different from the young people she met at the Institute for Self Development. She said that she was praying for Skipper. The young man was eventually sentenced to prison.

The attack had a deep effect upon Rosa's sense of personal safety, and she decided to move to the twenty-fifth floor of a gated and guarded high-rise complex overlooking the Detroit River. There she lived out the remainder of her days.

Rosa never gave up her activism. She had engaged in Black Power events in the 1970s and had demonstrated against apartheid at the South African embassy in Washington, D.C. She had also lobbied to make Martin Luther King Jr.'s birthday a national holiday. And then in 1995 eighty-two-year-old Rosa took part in the Million Man March.

Rosa died on October 24, 2005, fifty years after her historic act, and just three years before America's first black president was elected. She was ninety-two. Her coffin was laid in honor in the Capitol rotunda—"the first woman and second African American to be granted this honor,"[37] where forty thousand people came to say farewell.

Her funeral service in Detroit was attended by former President Clinton, then-Senator Barack Obama, and many other notable people. President George W. Bush honored her with what is perhaps the greatest honor of all when he ordered that a statue of Rosa Parks be created and put on permanent display in the U.S. Capitol's Statuary Hall. The legacy of her brave stand will go on forever in the lives she touched and changed. One example we may fittingly close with is that of Condoleeza Rice, who at a service for Rosa in Montgomery boldly said, "Without Mrs. Parks, I probably would not be standing here today as Secretary of State."[38]

SEVEN

Mother Teresa

1910–1997

L ast year I was in Skopje, the capital city of what is called by some the Republic of Macedonia and by others FYROM (Former Yugoslav Republic of Macedonia). I was there under the auspices of East-West Ministries of Dallas to speak to that nation's parliamentary leaders about the life of one of my heroes, William Wilberforce.[1]

One day during my visit, as I was walking through the center of the city, I was surprised to come upon a spot identified as the birthplace of another one of my heroes, Mother Teresa. I had completely forgotten that she was born in Skopje, and suddenly there I was standing on the very site where she had come into the world. The house itself had been destroyed in the great Skojpe earthquake of 1963, but the dimensions of the home were marked out on the pavement. It was incredibly tiny. Standing there I could hardly imagine that the baby born in such a tiny house would go on to become a saint and to inspire millions upon millions around the world.

She certainly inspired me. When I was invited to be the speaker at the National Prayer Breakfast in Washington, DC, in 2012,[2] I immediately thought of Mother Teresa, whose speech there in 1994 was the only one many people seemed to remember. It wasn't until I had to write my own speech that I watched hers online.[3]

Mother Teresa was so short that in the video her face is mostly obscured by the microphone, but the moral authority and palpable holiness of this tiny woman is astounding, even when viewed through the less-than-grand window of a YouTube video. When she spoke about abortion, telling President Bill Clinton to "stop killing" these children, to "give them to her," it inspired me to speak of the taking of unborn life in my own speech. It was the least I could do, feeling so unequal to the high honor of following in the footsteps of this extraordinary woman of God.

In modern times, few have had the impact Mother Teresa did. Her very name represented—and still represents—holiness and compassion to many around the world. Catholics, Protestants, Muslims, Hindus, and atheists all respected and loved her. She lived out the commands of Christ: love God, and love your neighbor as yourself. And she deliberately made some of the poorest people on earth her nearest neighbors.

Some years ago, passengers on a Pan Am flight were startled by an announcement from the jet's copilot. Emerging from the cockpit, he told them that they had a special guest on board: Mother Teresa of Calcutta, founder of the Missionaries of Charity, winner of the Nobel Peace Prize, and friend to everyone from destitute leprosy victims to Pope John Paul II.

The copilot pulled off his cap. If the passengers wanted to assist in Mother Teresa's work with the poor, he said, they could put money in his cap. He then walked up and down the aisles, and when he returned to the front, he had more than six hundred dollars to present to the tiny, elderly nun.[4]

On principle, Mother Teresa always bought economy class tickets but was routinely bumped up to first class. Flight attendants—who considered it a privilege to serve her—escorted her off the plane to the airport's VIP lounge and carried her luggage for her. It was an honor simply to be near her. She was a frail treasure that needed to be guarded carefully.

My old boss Chuck Colson, who founded Prison Fellowship and BreakPoint, greatly admired Mother Teresa. In fact, he corresponded with her and kept a plaque on his desk with one of her sayings: "Faithfulness, not success." When President Ronald Reagan was asked what he told Mother Teresa at the White House in 1986, he said he had listened instead; New York mayor Ed Koch said it was impossible to say no to her when she wanted something. Mother Teresa never thought she was too important to scrub toilets at the motherhouse in India; and she so disliked spending money on plane tickets that she wrote to one airline offering to work as a flight attendant in exchange for being allowed to fly free.

Mother Teresa had a playful side to her personality. Once, when she was invited to hear Mass at the Vatican with her friend Pope John Paul II, she decided to bring a priest along to meet him. But the Vatican had not invited the priest, and showing up uninvited to see the pope in his apartments is like showing up uninvited at the White House for a little chat with the president. It simply is not done; in fact, one could get arrested for doing so, or worse. But Mother Teresa got away with it, dragging the embarrassed priest through several layers of outraged security, right into the *sanctum sanctorum* of the pope's living room.

Her impact was so great that it wasn't unusual for a few minutes' conversation with Mother Teresa to change someone's life dramatically. Mother Teresa frequently asked strangers on the street for help—such as moving heavy boxes into one of her facilities for the poor. The strangers usually agreed, and when it dawned on them who it was they had assisted, they were overjoyed.

How did Mother Teresa go about loving her neighbors, and why did she love them so richly? Perhaps her vision can be summed up in the words of Matthew 25:34–40, which she quoted often:

> Then the King will say to those on His right hand, "Come, you blessed of My Father, inherit the kingdom prepared for you from the foundation of the world: for I was hungry and you gave Me food; I was thirsty and you gave Me drink; I was a stranger and you took Me in; I was naked and you clothed Me; I was sick and you visited Me; I was in prison and you came to Me."
>
> Then the righteous will answer Him, saying, "Lord, when did we see You hungry and feed You, or thirsty and give You drink? When did we see You a stranger and take You in, or naked and clothe You? Or when did we see You sick, or in prison, and come to You?" And the King will answer and say to them, "Assuredly, I say to you, inasmuch as you did it to one of the least of these My brethren, you did it to Me."

Mother Teresa said that she saw Jesus in every man, woman, or child she met, and she treated them accordingly. She thought the biggest problem on earth was being unloved; and if, in her exhaustion, all she could offer someone was a smile, she gave it.

She wanted to show the love of Christ in all she did—in helping the malnourished child and the woman dying in the gutter. To her, all these were simply "Jesus in His distressing disguise," as she put it. Because of this she was widely considered a saint during her lifetime, long before the Vatican made it official.

◆ ◆ ◆

The girl who would become Mother Teresa of Calcutta was born Gonxha Agnes Bojaxhiu on August 26, 1910, in Skopje, at that time part of the Ottoman Empire. Agnes's parents were Dranafile (Drana) and Nikola Bojaxhiu. She had an older brother, born in 1907, and an older sister, Aga, born in 1904.

The vast majority—90 percent—of the family's neighbors were Muslims; 10 percent, like the Bojaxhiu family, were Roman Catholics. Agnes's father was a partner in a construction company, a member of the community council, and a food importer, which meant frequent travel to far-flung lands.

Agnes's father died somewhat mysteriously when she was eight years old. The family thought it possible he had been poisoned by political or business adversaries but never found out for certain. In any event the family was instantly plunged into poverty, in part because Nikola's business partner had absconded with the company's assets. To pay the bills Agnes's mother took in sewing, but Agnes recalled that even facing hard times, her mother continued to look after the needs of the poor and sick in the neighborhood.

Agnes observed her mother each week bringing food to the home of a poor woman and even cleaning her house. She also took care of another woman whose body was covered in sores, and when a poor widow died, she took the woman's children into her own family. She was the model for the young girl who would one day become Mother Teresa.

Despite the loss of her father, Agnes recalled a happy childhood. Her family had always been very devout in their faith. Her mother took Agnes and the other children to church daily, and every evening the family gathered together to pray. But they also played and sang music each night. Both prayer and music were vital parts of their daily lives. Agnes attended a convent primary school and later went to a state school. She and her sister joined the choir of Sacred Heart Church, where Agnes learned to play the mandolin.

Although she suffered from a chronic cough due to weak lungs, Agnes was popular and fun-loving. She enjoyed reading and taking part in church youth group activities that included walks, concerts, and parties. She was an innate leader and organizer. Her parish priest, Father Jambrekovic, had a tremendous impact on Agnes's spiritual life.

Agnes was just twelve when she began to believe that God was calling her to the religious life. But how, she asked Father Jambrekovic, could she be absolutely certain that God wanted her to enter religious life? Joy, he responded, was the proof of the rightness of any endeavor.

Agnes was happy at home and didn't especially want to become a nun. But by the time she was eighteen, she firmly believed she was meant to "belong completely to God."[5]

Through Father Jambrekovic, Agnes learned about the mission work that the Society of Jesus was doing in India. Their inspiring letters about their work among Calcutta's poor and sick, along with their personal visits to Skopje and the enthusiasm Father Jambrekovic expressed for this work, inspired Agnes to join them.

Despite the fact she would have to leave her beloved family, Agnes chose to apply to the Sisters of Loreto, who were located in Ireland. When she told her mother what she intended to do, Drana decided to test her daughter's commitment and refused to give her consent to the plan. But Agnes stood firm. Following twenty-four hours of prayer, her mother told Agnes she could go.

On September 26, 1928, not knowing she would never again see her mother or sister, Agnes climbed aboard a train headed for Paris. There she submitted to an interview by Mother Eugene MacAvin, who ran Loreto House in Paris. She was then permitted to continue north to Dublin, where she would be entrusted to the care of Mother M. Raphael Deasy.

Agnes received her postulant's cap at Loreto Abbey in Rathfarnham, a Dublin suburb, on October 12, and spent the next six weeks learning English. She chose the name of Sister Mary Teresa of the Child Jesus, after Thérèse of Lisieux, the French Carmelite nun. Then, on December 1, she boarded a ship and set sail for India, where she would begin her lifelong service to God.

Sister Teresa's first sight of India—the city of Madras, now called Chennai—shocked her. The woman who would spend her life serving the poorest of the poor realized that she had no real idea what true poverty could look like. In a Catholic mission magazine article, she described the situation: "Many families live in the streets, along the city walls, even in places thronged with people. They are all virtually naked, wearing at best a ragged loincloth. . . . As we went along the street we chanced upon one family gathered around a dead relation, wrapped in worn red rags. . . . It was a horrifying scene. If our people could only see all this, they would stop grumbling about their own misfortunes and offer thanks to God for blessing them with such abundance."[6]

Sister Teresa and a fellow novitiate traveled to Calcutta on January 6, 1929, and a week later traveled to Darjeeling, where both formally became Loreto novices. Sister Teresa added the study of Hindi and Bengali to the English she had begun studying in Ireland. Her first job was teaching at the Loreto convent school, and she briefly assisted the nursing staff at a nearby medical station.

Another article Sister Teresa wrote for the Catholic mission magazine shows her growing concern for the deeply poor and sick. "Many have come from a distance, walking for as much as three miles," she wrote. "Their ears and feet covered in sores. They have lumps and lesions on their backs. Many stay home because they are too debilitated by tropical fever to come."[7]

"When a man brings an emaciated child to the medical station, she explains that he is afraid we will not take the child, and says, 'If you do not want him, I will throw him into the grass. The jackals will not turn up their noses at him.' My heart freezes. . . . With much pity and love I take the little one into my arms, and fold him in my apron."[8]

After her time in Darjeeling, Sister Teresa traveled to Calcutta's Loreto Convent, Entally, where she taught at two different schools— one, a boarding school for girls from broken homes or with other difficulties; the other, St. Mary's high school, where she taught geography and history to Bengali girls. Outside the walls of the convent compound, Sister Teresa also taught at St. Teresa's primary school, where her pupils were desperately poor. But while she was distressed by their poverty, she experienced great joy in teaching and loving the children, who called her *Ma*, the Bengali word for *mother*.

In 1937, at the age of twenty-seven, Sister Teresa made her final vows, pledging herself to a life of chastity, poverty, and obedience. Loreto nuns typically take on the title "Mother," and so from this point on, Agnes Bojaxhiu would be called "Mother Teresa."

In addition to her teaching duties, once a week Mother Teresa visited the poor, who lived in shacks in Calcutta's slums. Mixing with the poor, whom she called "wonderful people," reinforced what she had learned many years before at home: that one could be deeply happy despite the lack of material possessions.

The years of the Second World War brought great difficulties, including a famine that killed millions. During this time the numbers of orphans arriving at the convent increased, and the British took over the Entally compound, using it as a military hospital. Despite the danger from Japanese troops in nearby Burma, Mother Teresa refused to leave India. When the Bengali school was moved to a new location, she was promoted to headmistress. When the war ended, the sisters and their students moved back to the Entally convent.

In 1946 Mother Teresa's superiors feared she might succumb to tuberculosis because of her weak chest, so they insisted that she rest in bed several hours each day to preserve her strength—something she did with great reluctance, as she much preferred to stay busy. At the end of this period, Mother Teresa went on retreat in Darjeeling. On September 10, while traveling by train journey to the hill station, her life would change dramatically. She said that while she was riding along and praying, she heard God's call to leave the convent in which she had taught for some twenty years and go out into the streets to help the poorest of the poor. This date is now celebrated by the Missionaries of Charity as "Inspiration Day."

"The call of God to be a Missionary of Charity is the hidden treasure for me, for which I have sold all to purchase it," she later recalled. God was telling her, she said, "to leave the convent and help the poor while living among them. It was an order. To fail it would have been to break the faith."⁹

God continued to press this call on her mind and heart during the retreat, and Mother Teresa began to visualize how to implement this vision. The following month she confided in Father Van Exem and asked for his thoughts on her proposal to start a new congregation of nuns who would live among the poor.

This new congregation would take a special vow, in which they would rely entirely on God to provide for their needs, assuming, that is, anyone decided to join her in this challenging life. They would live in the same conditions in which the poor lived and would specifically seek to live out Christ's command from Matthew 25:35–36: "For I was hungry and you gave Me food; I was thirsty and you gave Me drink; I was a stranger and you took Me in; I was naked and you clothed Me; I was sick and you visited Me; I was in prison and you came to Me."

Father Van Exem suggested that Mother Teresa continue praying about this for a time, and then in January 1947 he told her to write to Archbishop Ferdinand Périer. In fact, he went to see the archbishop himself to lay out Mother Teresa's wishes. The archbishop was doubtful. After all, other orders were already helping the poor in Calcutta. The archbishop was also taken aback by Mother Teresa's desire to go out among the poor instead of letting the poor come to them. His instruction to Mother Teresa was that she wait for at least a year.

Finally in 1948 Mother Teresa was given permission to leave the convent for one year to see how she would fare living in the manner she had proposed. After that time the archbishop would decide whether she should continue. She rejoiced at the news and immediately went to a local bazaar to choose inexpensive saris for which her order would one day become famous. They were white, to represent purity, with stripes of blue, the color associated with Mary, the mother of Jesus. The saris would be worn over white habits.

On August 16 Mother Teresa left the Loreto convent to begin the work she had been praying about and envisioning for so long. She had just five rupees to her name and was leaving behind friends who would deeply miss her. She later wrote that leaving Loreto was her greatest sacrifice, "the most difficult thing I have ever done. It was much more difficult than to leave my family and country to enter religious life. Loreto, my spiritual training, my work there, meant everything to me."[10]

Mother Teresa first traveled to Patna, where the Medical Mission Sisters worked at the Holy Family Hospital, to spend three months studying the treatment for the diseases of the poor and malnourished. She knew she would need this training. When she returned to Calcutta, she began to search for an appropriate place to live and work. She was allowed to move into a little room in a building occupied by the Little Sisters of the Poor, nuns who served two hundred elderly poor in the city.

Then in December, Mother Teresa officially began what British journalist and admirer Malcolm Muggeridge called a work of "outrageous courage"—work that would occupy her time, energies, and love for the rest of her life. The first day she ventured into Calcutta's Motijhil slum and gathered together her first few children for "school" that met on a muddy patch of ground between huts. She taught the children the Bengali alphabet by drawing the letters into the mud and having the children watch and repeat the letters after her. The following day many more students came.

In her record of that time, Mother Teresa wrote, "Those who were not clean I gave a good wash in the tank. We had catechism after the first lesson in hygiene and their reading. . . . After needlework class we went to visit the sick."[11] She gave them milk at lunchtime and handed out soap as prizes. The first helper, who had once taught at St. Mary's, arrived to assist her.

Eventually, local well wishers who saw what she was doing began donating money and food, and Mother Teresa was able to rent two huts, one for her school, and the other for those who were sick and dying.

She had begun to realize that such a home was necessary in order to spare the dying from the indignity of passing away in the gutters, being gnawed on by rats. She wrote in her diary about helping an ill woman she found on the street get to the hospital. The woman was refused care because she could not pay. "She died on the street. I knew then that I must make a home for the dying, a resting place for people going to heaven. . . . We cannot let a child of God die like an animal in the gutter."[12]

Mother Teresa knew she could not stay at the Little Sisters of the Poor indefinitely; she needed to find a place to live closer to the slums in which she ministered, and where she could work in community with sisters who eventually—she hoped—would join the work. Father Van Exem found her a house owned by a lay member of the Legion of Mary. She could live in an empty room on its second floor, rent-free, and a large room on the third floor would be made available to any helpers who joined her. Inspecting Mother Teresa's small room, which then contained only a bench, a box, a chair, and an altar, the mother of the Little Sisters of the Poor dryly commented, "They cannot say that you left Loreto to become rich."[13] Nuns from Loreto eventually supplied Mother Teresa with a simple bed.

Mother Teresa began making frequent visits to local pharmacies— not to beg, but to ask, with her lovely smile, "Would you like to do something beautiful for God?" (The question would later become well known after British journalist Malcolm Muggeridge made a documentary about her titled *Something Beautiful for God*.) Of course the pharmacist would. And then she would hand him a list of medicines she needed for those she was assisting.

She was not so popular with the staffs of hospitals, who grew frustrated when they saw the nun pushing in a wheelchair, or transporting via rickshaw, or carrying in her arms various men, women, and children who were near death. The hospitals often refused to accept the would-be patients, who they knew would be unable to pay for treatment.

The work was hard, and at the beginning Mother Teresa was often lonely and sorely tempted to return to her beloved Loreto convent. On March 19, 1949, a few months after she had begun her work, one of her former students, Subashini Das, arrived at Mother Teresa's lodgings, eager to help. Eventually this young Bengali woman became an aspirant, taking the given name of her beloved teacher: Agnes. In time she became Sister Agnes. Soon another of Mother Teresa's former pupils, Magdalena Gomes, announced she wanted to join the work, and she moved in with Mother Teresa. She later became Sister Gertrude. Before long two more former students joined them. Mother Teresa's teachings about the need to care for the poor had made their mark.

The realization that serving the poor was hard work also made its mark, although what these nuns did they did with joy, knowing that it was a privilege to serve God by serving "the least of these." They worked eight hours each day, with the exception of Sundays and Thursdays. There were breaks for meals, Mass, prayer, housework, rest, and reflection. They all performed the same work Mother Teresa did: going into the slums to provide food and simple medical care, visiting the elderly, giving comfort to the abandoned, and teaching children their letters and proper hygiene. They also knocked on doors asking for money and leftover food to support the work. Many were happy to give, but not everyone was friendly or approved of the way the nuns were living, including some fellow Christians.

Eventually Mother Teresa asked Calcutta city authorities for a building for the sick and the dying. The city was well aware of the extraordinary work she was doing, and they gave her a hostel. The building was next door to a temple devoted to Kali, the fearsome and many-armed Hindu goddess of death. Pilgrims to the temple had once stayed in the building, but now it was abandoned and filthy. A delighted Mother Teresa, aided by her helpers, cleaned the place up and renamed it Nirmal Hriday, a Bengali term meaning "Place of the Immaculate Heart." There the sisters would take in the sick and the dying, wash them of the vomit and filth that often covered them, treat their wounds, feed them, and allow them a clean place to die while feeling loved and wanted and in the presence of a gentle, smiling face.

At death each person was allowed the rituals of his faith, whether Christian, Hindu, or Muslim.

Not surprisingly some of the more radical Hindus were not pleased that Christian nuns were working on the premises of a Hindu goddess and perhaps even proselytizing Hindus. So when Mother Teresa took over the building, violent protests followed. One day a Hindu leader gathered a mob of young people, armed with stones, to help him drive out Mother Teresa and her helpers. When she heard the hubbub outside, she came out the front door and courageously and calmly approached the mob. She soon learned who was leading this angry crowd and addressed him directly, inviting the Hindu leader to come inside and see for himself what the sisters were doing.

When he came out a short time later, the mob, still waiting for his instructions, asked him if they could begin what they had come to do—drive out the nuns by force. "Yes, you can," the man replied, "but only when your sisters and your mothers do what those Sisters are doing in there."[14]

During the first year of Mother Teresa's work with the poor, ten young women joined her, and by 1950 she had devised a constitution for the Missionaries of Charity—the name God had given her when she first heard her "call within a call." In the first and in every subsequent Missionaries of Charity chapel hangs a crucifix and the words "I thirst." As the journalist and historian David Aikman explained in his book *Great Souls*, "These are, of course, the real words of Christ on the cross. But to Mother Teresa they have always expressed Christ's desire, indeed His yearning, for us to love Him."[15]

Mother Teresa made it clear that the helpers—later they were called novices—were expected to be cheerful as they worked. She was determined that the members of the order would live as simply as the poor. Each morning, the nuns washed themselves and their clothing in buckets of water. They used ashes to clean their teeth, and they used the same tiny bar of soap to wash their bodies and their saris.

But with more and more helpers joining them, it became necessary to find a larger place in which to live. In 1953, after much prayer, Mother Teresa and Sister Gertrude approached Dr. Islam, a retired Muslim magistrate who had decided to move to Pakistan. His property was made up of two houses enclosing a central courtyard in the noisy heart of Calcutta. He had not mentioned his plans to anyone and was astonished when Mother Teresa brought up the possibility of buying his house. He sold it to them for far less than it was worth, and to this day it remains the motherhouse of the Missionaries of Charity. From their new home, the sisters looked out onto the streets of Calcutta, filled with pedestrians, rickshaws, and the sounds of busy traffic.

One thing that distinguished Mother Teresa as someone who truly believed in the everyday reality of God was her determination to live in complete reliance on him—meaning that she expected miracles. And there were many of them. One day the community ran out of food. Answering a knock on the door, they found a woman holding bags of rice. The woman informed them that some "inexplicable impulse" had brought her to them with the rice. It was just enough for their evening meal.[16]

Another time, in preparation for a new arrival, the sisters decided to make a mattress, which was their custom, but they ran out of cotton cloth to finish the job. When she learned of it, Mother Teresa offered to give them the fabric from her own pillow, but the sisters were reluctant to accept, feeling that she needed to have a comfortable pillow to rest on after her long day's work. But while she was insisting, there was a knock at the door. Answering it, the sisters found an Englishman standing there with a mattress under his arm. He told them that he was returning to England, and it had occurred to him that the sisters might need it. In these small ways, God assured the sisters that he was with them in their work. Each such miracle gave them tremendous encouragement.

On another occasion the sisters had no food with which to feed the seven thousand people dependent upon them over the next two days. In a "coincidence" that is simply inexplicable, the government shut down the local schools for those days and donated all the bread that would have been fed to the schoolchildren to the Missionaries of Charity.

On April 12, 1953, Mother Teresa and the first group of sisters took their final vows as Missionaries of Charity. The number of helpers continued to grow as doctors, nurses, and others volunteered their services. The sisters set up dispensaries to deal with the many diseased and malnourished people they were helping. Those in need included many Hindu refugees who had been forced out of Pakistan after the British "partition," which created the nation of Pakistan out of what had been the British India Empire.

In 1955 the Missionaries of Charity opened their first home for sick and unwanted children, Shishu Bhavan, not far from the motherhouse. It was the first of many more to come. Among the babies brought to the sisters were some who had literally been dumped in garbage cans or drains. Most of the older children who came to them suffered from tuberculosis and malnutrition.

Mother Teresa visited the children's home herself each day, taking particular interest in babies whose health was so precarious that they were likely to die soon. Wrapping the child in a blanket, she would hand him to a helper and simply instruct her to love the child until he died. She felt it absolutely central to her mission that no child should die without having experienced love. Even if tiny babies brought to them died within the hour, Mother Teresa insisted that they must die "beautifully." One of the helpers, who had been asked to love a dying baby, held the child and hummed a Brahms lullaby to him until he died that evening. Three decades later the woman still recalled how the tiny infant had pressed his little body against hers.

Of course not all the children died, and Mother Teresa taught those who regained their health at Shishu Bhavan a skill, such as typing, carpentry, or needlework, so that they would be able to get a job instead of having to beg on the streets. Others were sent to schools, and well-heeled sponsors, both in India and in other countries, paid their school fees. Families of the same faith adopted some of the children.

Mother Teresa also worked to end abortion by writing to clinics, police stations, and hospitals. The sisters made posters with this message, and young mothers began showing up day and night with babies they could not afford to keep. Childless couples were delighted to adopt many of these "unwanted" babies.

Malnourished children and the destitute dying were not the only people in whom Mother Teresa saw Christ in his "distressing disguise." In Calcutta alone, because of cramped conditions and the lack of adequate food and proper medical care, some thirty thousand people were afflicted with leprosy. Ignorance about this frightening disease made the problem worse, leading sufferers to hide it as long as possible for fear that their employers would fire them and their families reject them. So Mother Teresa opened a leper asylum in the Gobra district outside of Calcutta. When the government forced her to evacuate the patients as part of a development plan, she embarked on a fund-raising scheme, and in 1957, thanks to the generosity of wealthy Hindus and others—including the donation of an ambulance from the United States—she opened a mobile leprosy clinic.

The mobile clinic was a great improvement over Mother Teresa's original idea of building a home in which lepers could receive treatment, because patients could be treated in their own homes and, if they had a job, could continue working. Within a few months the Missionaries of Charity were treating six hundred lepers. Mother Teresa was insistent that—for the sake of their dignity—the lepers in treatment be taught skills, such as carpentry, making shoes, or sewing their own clothing, so they could be self-sufficient.

For those who would never be cured or who would never again be able to find work in the outside world, Mother Teresa built dozens of small houses and a hospital on land outside Calcutta that had been donated by the Indian government. The hospital was funded in part by raffling off a limousine given to her by Pope Paul VI following his visit to India. This home was called Shanti Nagar, meaning "The Place of Peace."

◆ ◆ ◆

Catholic canon law required ten years to elapse before the Missionaries of Charity would be allowed to open additional houses elsewhere in India. But the archbishop relaxed this rule by a year, allowing the congregation to begin expanding in 1959, nine years into the probationary period. In short order they set up houses in Delhi, Ranchi, Jhansi, and Mumbai.

In 1965 people beyond India began asking the Missionaries of Charity to come to them. Mother Teresa was asked to open a house in faraway Venezuela, which she did. On July 15 of that year, she met with Pope Paul VI, and three years later he invited Mother Teresa to open a house in Rome too.

As a child Mother Teresa had dreamed of traveling the world, and now she seemed to be on the road constantly, opening one house after another in such places as Tanzania, Ceylon, Australia, Yemen, Peru, Jordan, London, and New York.

In Western cities the needs were quite different than they were in the poverty-stricken places of the developing world. Drug and alcohol addiction were often the problems she had to deal with. In London, Mother Teresa was with a drug addict who had taken an overdose and died before her eyes. Her heart went out to alcoholics and mentally ill people, who even in wealthy countries were tragically left to fend for themselves. It was in the affluent West that Mother Teresa began to realize the extent of what she called "spiritual poverty." During a visit to London, she observed, "Here you have the Welfare State. Nobody need starve. But there is a different poverty. The poverty of the spirit, of loneliness and being unwanted."[17]

In 1968 Muggeridge became taken with Mother Teresa and decided to interview her for the BBC. This was the first time Mother Teresa was introduced to the world on a large scale. But she was nervous during the interview and gave simple answers to his polished questions. In his book, *Something Beautiful for God*, Muggeridge said that the "verdict on the Mother Teresa interview was that, technically, it was barely usable, and there was for a while some doubt as to whether it was good enough for showing at all except late at night."

In the end, the program aired on a Sunday evening. "[T]he response," he wrote, "was greater than I have known to any comparable programme, both in mail and in contributions of money for Mother Teresa's work. All of them said approximately the same thing—this woman spoke to me as no one ever has, and I feel I must help her."[18] When the program aired again not long afterward, the response was greater yet, with twenty thousand pounds pouring in for the little nun with the simple answers.

Muggeridge traveled to Calcutta in 1969, hoping to persuade Mother Teresa to allow him to film her and her sisters at work among the poor. She reluctantly agreed. Part of the filming was to be done in the Home for the Dying. The resulting film contained an unexpected and luminous miracle. As Muggeridge explained:

This Home for the Dying is dimly lit by small windows high up in the walls, and Ken [the cameraman] was adamant that filming was quite impossible there. We had only one small light with us, and to get the place adequately lighted in the time at our disposal was quite impossible. It was decided that, nonetheless, Ken should have a go, but by way of insurance he took, as well, some film in an outside courtyard where some of the inmates were sitting in the sun. In the processed film, the part taken inside was bathed in a particularly beautiful soft light, whereas the part taken outside was rather dim and confused.

How to account for this? Ken has all along insisted that, technically speaking, the result is impossible. To prove the point, on his next filming expedition—to the Middle East—he used some of the same stock in a similarly poor light, with completely negative results. He offers no explanation. . . . I myself am absolutely convinced that the technically unaccountable light is, in fact, the Kindly Light

Newman refers to in his well-known exquisite hymn. . . . Mother Teresa's Home for the Dying is overflowing with love, as one senses immediately on entering it. This love is luminous, like the halos artists have seen and made visible round the heads of the saints.[19]

Mother Teresa had a tremendous impact on this lifelong skeptic, who became a Christian in his sixties and a Catholic when he was seventy-nine, largely through Mother Teresa's influence. Her effect on him is clear in a passage in *Something Beautiful for God*. Muggeridge wrote that he dropped her off one morning at a Calcutta train station, and "when the train began to move, and I walked away, I felt as though I were leaving behind me all the beauty and all the joy in the universe."[20]

◆ ◆ ◆

Mother Teresa's increasing fame brought criticism from those who thought they knew more about helping the poor than she did. They wondered why she did not attack the institutional structures that caused poverty. Why did she not reorganize the Missionaries of Charity in such a way that more people could be helped? Why did she not condemn dictators? Couldn't governments, with all their vast resources, do a better job helping the poor than a congregation of nuns? To all these critics Mother Teresa responded that God required her to do small things with great love; that while government welfare programs exist for quite admirable purposes, "Christian love is for a person."[21]

"I do not add up," she noted. "I only subtract from the total number of poor or dying. With children one dollar saves a life. . . . So we use ourselves to save what we can. . . . Every small act of love for the unwanted and the poor is important to Jesus."[22]

Others criticized Mother Teresa for not being more willing to witness to the teachings of the Church, not realizing the fine line Mother Teresa had to walk as a Christian missionary in a Hindu country. As well, she preferred to let the work itself do the witnessing. As she frequently told her sisters, quoting the words of Jesus: "Let them see your good works and glorify your father who is in heaven."[23]

The Missionaries of Charity continued to grow, even during a time when vocations for other religious orders were decreasing. It seemed there was something strangely compelling about the call to great poverty and a hard life aiding the poorest of the poor. In the 1980s and '90s, the Missionaries of Charity were able to open houses even in Communist and formerly Communist nations.

In 1963, because there were some things that could be better accomplished by men than women, a new branch of the congregation, the Missionary Brothers of Charities, was begun. A few years later the International Association of Co-Workers of Mother Teresa came into being, allowing thousands of laypeople around the globe to join the work. The Missionaries of Charity Contemplative Sisters was founded in 1977, and the Missionaries of Charity Contemplative Brothers was begun three years later. In 1984 the Missionaries of Charity Fathers joined the work.

◆ ◆ ◆

As the years passed, Mother Teresa received recognition and awards, which she always accepted on behalf of those she served. Documentaries were made of her life and work, and the famous—including sports stars, film celebrities, and Princess Diana—began to beat a path to her door to meet this woman many considered a living saint and to ask her blessing. Mother Teresa treated them just as she treated Calcutta's poor, with warmth and compassion. And she reminded one and all that taking care of the poor and hungry was nothing heroic or extraordinary. She referred to it as "a simple duty for you and for me."[24]

In 1979 one of the world's greatest honors was bestowed on Mother Teresa when she was awarded the Nobel Peace Prize. She decided that she would travel to Oslo, Norway, to accept the prize in person. But in her typical fashion, even in this highly secular nation Mother Teresa did not hesitate to proclaim her faith to the gathering of well-dressed guests, which included Norway's royal family. Jesus, she announced, "died on the cross to show that greater love, and He died for you and for me and for that leper and for that man dying of hunger and that naked person lying in the street. . . . And we read that in the Gospel very clearly: 'love as I have loved you; as I love you; as the Father has loved me, I love you.'"

She spoke of the spiritual poverty of wealthy nations where aging relatives are pushed into nursing homes, relatives who suffer emotional pain because they are seldom visited. She spoke of parents who were too busy working to pay attention to their children. And then she took direct aim at the violence of abortion in a country that had not only legalized it but also provided state funds to pay for what she regarded as nothing less than the murder of a human child:

> The greatest destroyer of peace today. Because if a mother can kill her own child—what is left for me to kill you and you kill me—there is nothing between. . . . Today, millions of unborn children are being killed—and we say nothing . . . nobody speaks of the millions of little ones who have been conceived with the same life as you and I. . . . We allow it. To me, the nations who have legalized abortion, they are the poorest nations. They are afraid of the little one! They are afraid of the unborn child, and the child must die because they don't want to feed one more child, to educate one more child.

She reminded her unsmiling audience of the humanity of the unborn baby:

> It was that unborn child that recognized the presence of Jesus when Mary came to visit Elizabeth, her cousin. As we read in the gospel, the moment Mary came into the house, the little one in the womb of his mother leaped with joy, recognizing the Prince of Peace. And

so today, let us here make a strong resolution: We are going to save every little child, every unborn child, give them a chance to be born.

We are fighting abortion with adoption. And the good God has blessed the work so beautifully. . . . We have saved thousands of children, and thousands of children have found a home where they are loved and wanted . . . and so today, I ask you: Let us all pray that we have the courage to stand by the unborn child.[25]

One can only imagine the reaction of the sophisticates on the Nobel committee, who had intended to grandly bestow one of the world's highest honors on this little nun for her good work among the poor, and who in the crowning apex of the ceremony found themselves being soundly rebuked for their embrace of a great moral evil.

Mother Teresa reprised this peroration fifteen years later, when she was invited to be the guest speaker at the National Prayer Breakfast in Washington, DC. Addressing President Bill Clinton and Hillary Clinton, Vice President Al Gore and Tipper Gore, members of the U.S. House and Senate, religious leaders, and the very court that had put their legal imprimatur on the violent act that had taken the lives of millions of unborn American babies, Mother Teresa said: "But I feel that the greatest destroyer of peace today is abortion, because Jesus said, if you receive a little child you receive me. So every abortion is the denial of receiving Jesus—is the neglect of receiving Jesus."[26]

What many news outlets left out of their coverage of her speech was the fact that, at this point, the audience burst into sustained applause. If you watch the speech on YouTube, you may see the cameras pulling back during the seemingly unending applause to reveal the Clintons and the Gores, well-known for their strong defense of abortion rights, stiff and uncomfortable on either side of Mother Teresa, refusing to applaud what she had just said and surely wishing they were somewhere else.

n 1975 the Missionaries of Charity celebrated its Silver Jubilee. These twenty-five years had been "joyful and hard," Mother Teresa wrote in a letter to those who had shared in the work. "We have worked together for Jesus and with Jesus. . . . Let us thank God for all gifts and promise [that] we will make our Society something beautiful for God."[27]

In January 1985 she traveled to China, visiting a Beijing home for the elderly and a factory where handicapped workers were employed. That year she also became aware of the AIDS epidemic in America and of how its victims were often abandoned by friends and family and left to die miserable deaths alone. While some Christians may have privately considered that these mostly homosexual men were reaping the consequences of their own behavior and thus deserved little sympathy, Mother Teresa, observing their suffering, saw Jesus in yet another "distressing disguise." She opened New York's first hospice for AIDS victims in Greenwich Village.

In 1990 Mother Teresa turned eighty and resigned, with considerable relief, as superior general of the Missionaries of Charity. It was something she had wanted to do for some years. She had many health problems caused by exhaustion, flare-ups of malaria, and failing vision, and she had suffered various injuries. She had a stroke in her midsixties and in 1981 had learned she had a serious heart condition, something she insisted be kept secret. In 1989 an external pacemaker had been fitted; it was later replaced with an internal one.

In a letter to all those involved in the work of the Missionaries of Charity, Mother Teresa offered her prayers, love, and gratitude "for all you have been and have done all these forty years to share in the joy of loving each other and the Poorest of the Poor. . . . Beautiful are the ways of God if we allow him to use us as he wants."[28]

But her resignation, which had been announced by Pope John Paul II, was dramatically short-lived. When she was once again reelected by the Missionaries of Charity General Council to lead the congregation, Mother Teresa accepted it as God's will. Now stooped with age, she continued to travel on behalf of the poorest of the poor and to attend the professions of Missionaries of Charity sisters making first or final vows.

In 1997, Mother Teresa was finally allowed to step down as superior general for the Missionaries of Charity. Elected to take her place was Sister Nirmala, a Hindu convert.

On August 26, Mother Teresa celebrated her eighty-seventh birthday at the motherhouse in Calcutta. Time was running out for this passionate servant of Jesus. A few days later, on August 31, her friend, thirty-six-year-old Princess Diana, died in a car crash in Paris. Shocking as it was, this became the focus of the whole world's attention for several weeks. Mother Teresa told the press she would pray for the princess, who, she said, had a special love for the world's poor. But on September 5, while the world was still in the midst of mourning Princess Diana's untimely death, Mother Teresa—thousands of miles from the funeral frenzy in London—quietly passed away, or went home to God, as she would have put it.

India, mourning the loss of a woman loved by the world, gave Mother Teresa a state funeral. Her body lay in state at St. Thomas's Church, visited by hundreds of thousands of mourners, from the very poor to those occupying high places in the world, including the duchess of Kent, representing Queen Elizabeth; Hillary Clinton, representing the United States; and Bernadette Chirac, representing her husband, Jacques Chirac, the president of France. All wanted to bid farewell to the woman who, for many of them, had been the personification of love. Pope John Paul II sent a message to be read at her funeral, urging others to continue the work Mother Teresa had begun.

This work, at the time of her death, amounted to a tremendous achievement. The woman who had heard God's voice on a train some fifty years before had left behind a huge legacy: four thousand sisters serving Jesus around the world, more than four hundred brothers, plus the many Missionaries of Charity Fathers, Lay Missionaries of Charity, and other volunteers, all carrying on the work to which she had devoted her life.

Mother Teresa was laid to rest at the motherhouse in Calcutta, surrounded by the sounds of the city—trams and traffic, rickshaw bells, and passing parades—which had served as background music to her magnificent work for decades. In October 2003 she was beatified by Pope John Paul II.

————— ◆ ◆ ◆ —————

In the years following Mother Teresa's death, some of her private letters to her spiritual adviser, Father Van Exem, and Archbishop Ferdinand Périer, were published. Some of their contents surprised those who had come to know and love her. As CNN put it, "The world is discovering a new Mother Teresa—one at times fraught with painful feelings of abandonment by God."[29]

Among the fascinating details: Mother Teresa had always stated that on Inspiration Day, she had not had a vision. But her writings revealed what she had obviously felt unable to share publicly during her lifetime—that for several months she experienced a period of union with God during which she heard a series of interior locutions in which Jesus called her to carry him into the "holes" of the poor, to bring the light of faith to those living in darkness, and so bring joy to the suffering heart of Jesus. . . . She also "saw" a series of progressively intensifying scenes of an immense crowd of all kinds of people in great sorrow and suffering, eventually covered in darkness. Most surprising of all was Mother Teresa's admission that she "no longer felt the proximity of God in the same way that she had for that privileged period in 1946 and 1947." She experienced "spiritual dryness, the profound pain of God's apparent absence despite her great thirst for him, and a lack of sensible consolation."[30]

And yet, many who knew her well—who witnessed her joy, her smile, and her work—would have been puzzled by her revelations.

"It is clear that Mother Teresa's inner (and outer) world was a place in which the brilliance of God's light and the bleakness of man's darkness met and mingled—from which her victorious light only shone the brighter," wrote biographer Father Joseph Langford. "What emerged from that inner struggle was a light in no way lessened by her bearing the cloak of humanity's pain, but a light all the more resplendent, and all the more approachable . . . a light entirely accessible to the poorest, beckoning to God's brightness all who share in the common human struggle."[31]

Those who made the decision to publish her words had done so in order to increase not only the world's understanding of Mother Teresa but also the true meaning of holiness.

—————◆◆◆—————

Mother Teresa was considered a saint because she was seen to personify an ideal: to love God, and to love one's neighbor. And yet, what she did was so simple that each one of us can do it—in fact, must do it, if we are to obey the command of Christ: to feed the hungry, care for the sick, invite the stranger in, clothe the naked, visit those in prison, and quench the thirst of those who simply need a cup of water.

It was constant prayer that gave Mother Teresa the strength to keep going and caused her to produce such tremendous fruit. And it is prayer that must undergird all efforts to obey God, because as Mother Teresa of Calcutta would be the first to say, obedience is not always easy. In fact, without God's help, it is impossible.

As Langford put it, Mother Teresa plunged, "for love's sake, into the dark homes and hearts of the poor. May her gentle, guiding light born of the heart of the Almighty be yours: A light that flies not from darkness—but ever towards it."[32]

Acknowledgments

I am first of all grateful to all the women who after reading my *Seven Men* book encouraged me to write this book. And I am deeply grateful to all those people who helped me write it. I am most grateful to my friend Anne Morse for helping me research a number of the chapters and for writing the initial drafts of those chapters. Thanks also to Karen Swallow Prior for writing *Fierce Convictions*, without which my knowledge of Hannah More could not be what it is. Finally, I am grateful to Joel Miller for encouraging me to write this book for Thomas Nelson, and for educating me about the existence of the extraordinary Maria Skobtsova, without whom this book might well have included a chapter on Shirley "Cha-cha" Muldowney, Totie Fields, or Moms Mabley. *Soli Deo Gloria.*

Notes

INTRODUCTION

1. Eric Metaxas, *Bonhoeffer: Pastor, Martyr, Prophet, Spy* (Nashville: Thomas Nelson, 2010).
2. Eric Metaxas, *Amazing Grace: William Wilberforce and the Heroic Campaign to End Slavery* (New York: Harper San Francisco, 2007).
3. Eric Metaxas, *Seven Men and the Secret to Their Greatness* (Nashville: Thomas Nelson, 2013).
4. For more information, please visit www.socratesinthecity.com.
5. Alice von Hildebrand, *The Privilege of Being a Woman* (Ypsilanti, MI: Veritas Press, 2002).
6. Alice von Hildebrand, *Man and Woman: A Divine Invention* (Ave Maria, FL: Sapientia Press of Ave Maria University, 2010).
7. For a link to that interview, visit www.socratesinthecity.com.

CHAPTER ONE: JOAN OF ARC

1. *The Passion of Joan of Arc* was directed by Carl Theodor Dreyer and stars Renée Maria Falconetti. The 1928 silent film is based on the transcript of her trial in 1431 and is a widely acclaimed work of cinema.

2. Patricia Moynagh, "Beyond Just War: Joan of Arc and Fighting Without Malice," July 2014, http://web.isanet.org/Web/Conferences/FLACSO-ISA%20BuenosAires%202014/Archive/22fa5cfc-9c9c-4241-a910-6e8bfe9ff74f.pdf.

3. Mark Twain, *Joan of Arc* (San Francisco: Ignatius Press, 2007), 92.

4. Regine Pernoud and Marie-Véronique Clin, *Joan of Arc: Her Story,* ed. Bonnie Wheeler, trans. and rev. Jeremy du Quesnay Adams (New York: St. Martin's Press, 1999), 23.

5. Hilaire Belloc, *Joan of Arc* (Charlotte, NC: Neumann Press, 1997), Kindle edition location 255.

6. Ibid.

7. Ibid., Kindle edition location 305.

8. Ibid., Kindle edition location 358.

9. Ibid., Kindle edition location 367.

10. Pernoud and Clin, *Joan of Arc,* 31.

11. Belloc, *Joan of Arc,* Kindle edition location 404.

12. Peggy McCracken.

13. Kelly DeVries, *Joan of Arc: A Military Leader* (Stroud, Gloucester: The History Press, 2011), 63.

14. Ibid., 64.

15. Pernoud and Clin, *Joan of Arc,* 37–38.

16. Ibid., 39.

17. Walter Adams, "April 29—Joan Arrives to Orleans and Crossly Scolds Dunois, the Bastard of Orleans," *Le Royaume des Ste. Jehanne et Ste. Thérèse,* http://joanandtherese.com/2010/07/31/april-29-joan-arrives-to-orleans-and-crossly-scolds-dunois-the-bastard-of-orleans.

18. Walter Adams, "May 5—Feast of the Ascension—Joan Refuses Battle in Honor of the Holy Day—but Sends a Final Ultimatum," *Le Royaume des Ste. Jehanne et Ste. Thérèse,* http://joanandtherese.com/2010/07/31/may-5-feast-of-the-ascension-joan-refuses-battle-in-honor-of-the-holy-day-but-sends-a-final-ultimatum.

19. Pernoud and Clin, *Joan of Arc,* 43.

20. Ibid., 44.

21. Ibid., 45.

22. Walter Adams, "May 6—Joan's Bravery in the Face of Confusion at Iles-aux-Toiles Provokes an Ill-Fated English Attack," *Le Royaume des Ste. Jehanne et Ste. Thérèse*, http://joanandtherese.com/2010/07/31/may-6-joans-bravery-in-the-face-of-confusion-at-iles-aux-toiles-provokes-an-ill-fated-english-attack.

23. Belloc, *Joan of Arc*, Kindle edition location 582.

24. Ibid., Kindle edition location 594.

25. Ibid.

26. Ibid., Kindle edition location 623.

27. Pernoud and Clin, *Joan of Arc*, 58.

28. Belloc, *Joan of Arc*, Kindle edition location 653.

29. Ibid., Kindle edition location 653.

30. DeVries, *Joan of Arc*, 133.

31. Belloc, *Joan of Arc*, Kindle edition location 786.

32. "Joan of Arc's Letter to the citizens of Rheims (August 5, 1429)," *Joan of Arc Archive*, http://archive.joan-of-arc.org/joanofarc_letter_aug_5_1429.html.

33. Pernoud and Clin, *Joan of Arc*, 89.

34. Ibid., 87.

35. Ibid.

36. Ibid., 96.

37. Belloc, *Joan of Arc*, Kindle edition location 993.

38. "Third Public Examination," *Saint Joan of Arc Center*, www.stjoan-center.com/Trials/sec03.html.

39. Belloc, *Joan of Arc*, Kindle edition location 1007.

40. Pernoud and Clin, *Joan of Arc*, 129.

41. Penelope Duckworth, "Saint Martha and Saint Joan: Proposals for the Commemoration of Two Women Who Shaped the History of Their Times," Episcopal Women's Caucus, www.episcopalwomenscaucus.org/ruach/GeneralConvention2006_vol26_3/06SaintMartha.html.

42. "Deliberations Held on May 9th, 12th and 19th and the Final Session and Sentence and Recantation," St. Joan of Arc Center, www.stjoan-center.com/Trials/sec20.html.

43. Pernoud and Clin, *Joan of Arc*, 130–131.

44. Ibid., 131.

45. Steven Kanehl, *I Was Born for This: Devoted to God Whatever the Cost* (Mustang, OK: Tate Publishing, 2008).

46. Pernoud and Clin, *Joan of Arc*, 132.
47. Robert R. Edgar, Neil J. Hackett, and George F. Jewsbury, *Civilization Past and Present* (New York: Longman, 2005), 2:435.
48. Steven R. Kanehl , "Jehanne la Pucelle: A Mini Biography," *Saint Joan of Arc Center,* www.stjoan-center.com/time_line/part10.html.
49. Pernoud and Clin, *Joan of Arc*, 133.
50. Belloc, *Joan of Arc*, Kindle edition location 1062.
51. Pernoud and Clin, *Joan of Arc*, 135.
52. Ibid., 136.
53. Allen Williamson, "Biography of Joan of Arc," *Saint Joan of Arc Center,* http://archive.joan-of-arc.org/joanofarc_short_biography.html.
54. "Joan of Arc, French National Heroe: A Theology for Mankind's Liberation," http://dbr-radio.com/joan-of-arc-theology.html.

CHAPTER TWO: SUSANNA WESLEY

1. Eric Metaxas, *Amazing Grace: William Wilberforce and the Heroic Campaign to End Slavery* (New York: Harper San Francisco, 2007), 168.
2. Such events give us some background in understanding why the Founding Fathers of the United States gave religious liberty such a prominent position, making it "the first freedom" by putting it first in the Bill of Rights.
3. Arnold A. Dallimore, *Susanna Wesley: The Mother of John and Charles Wesley* (Grand Rapids: Baker Book House, 1993), 14.
4. John. A. Newton, "Samuel Annesley (1620–1696)," *Proceedings of the Wesley Historical Society,* Sept. 1985, 45:39, www.biblicalstudies.org.uk/pdf/whs/45–2.pdf.
5. Susanna Wesley, *The Complete Writings*, ed. Charles Wallace, Jr. (Oxford: Oxford University Press, 1997), 99.
6. Luke Tyerman, *The Life and Times of the Rev. Samuel Wesley, M.A., Rector of Epworth, and Father of the Revs. John and Charles Wesley, the Founders of the Methodists* (London: Simpkin, Marshall & Co.), 251.
7. Wesley, *The Complete Writings*, 35–36.
8. Ibid., 37.
9. Ibid., 210.
10. John Kirk, *The Mother of the Wesleys*, vol. 1 (Cincinnati: Poe and Hitchcock, 1865), 161 (Available through Theclassics.us.).
11. Ibid., 151.

12. Dallimore, *Susanna Wesley,* 57–58.
13. Kathy McReynolds, *Susanna Wesley* (Ada, MI: Bethany House, 1998), 75.
14. Ibid., 76.
15. Ibid., 82.
16. Ibid., 76.
17. John Wesley, *The Journal of John Wesley,* vol. 1 (London: J. Kershaw, 1827), 371.
18. Ibid., 371–372.
19. E. V. Lucas, ed., *Her Infinite Variety: A Feminine Portrait Gallery* (University of California Libraries, 1908), 184.
20. Adam Clarke, *Memoirs of the Wesley Family* (London: J. & T. Clarke, 1823), 104. (Available through Ulan Press.)
21. Dallimore, *Susanna Wesley,* 67.
22. Clarke, *Memoirs of the Wesley Family,* 94.
23. Wesley, *The Complete Writings,* 65–66.
24. Dallimore, *Susanna Wesley,* 101.
25. John Wesley, *The Works of the Reverend John Wesley, a.m.,* vol. 3 (New York: J. Emory and B. Waugh, 1831), 265. (Available through Ulan Press.)
26. John Wesley, *The Works of the Rev. John Wesley, vol. 1* (London: The Confernece-Office, 1809), 39.
27. Susanna Wesley, *The Prayers of Susanna Wesley,* ed. W. L. Doughty (Grand Rapids: Zondervan, 1984), vii.
28. Ibid., 17.
29. Ibid., 19.
30. Ibid., 40.
31. Ibid., 3.
32. Ibid.
33. Dallimore, *Susanna Wesley,* 81.
34. McReynolds, *Susanna Wesley,* 54.
35. Ibid.
36. Mary Beth Crain, *Haunted Christmas: Yuletide Ghosts and Other Spooky Holiday Happenings* (Guilford, CT: Globe Pequot Press, 2010), 113–114.
37. Eliza Clarke, *Susanna Wesley,* Classic Reprint Series (London: Forgotten Books, 2012), 121.

38. John Fletcher Hurst, *John Wesley the Methodist* (New York: Eaton & Mains; Cincinnati: Jennings & Pye, 1903), 46.

39. Clarke, *Susanna Wesley*, 125.

40. Dallimore, *Susanna Wesley*, 91.

41. Ibid., 93.

42. Clarke, *Susanna Wesley*, 63–64.

43. Dallimore, *Susanna Wesley*, 132.

44. Ibid., 102.

45. Arthur Quiller-Couch, *Hetty Wesley* (London and New York: Harper and Brothers, 1903), 35–36.

46. Dallimore, *Susanna Wesley*, 113.

47. Ibid., 117.

48. "John Wesley and His Wife (part 2)," *Church History Blog*, https://lexloiz.wordpress.com/2010/03/19/john-wesley-and-his-wife-part-2/.

49. Dallimore, *Susanna Wesley*, 148.

50. "John Wesley the Methodist, Chapter VII—The New Birth," *Wesley Center Online*, http://wesley.nnu.edu/john-wesley/john-wesley-the-methodist/chapter-vii-the-new-birth/.

51. Christian Classics Ethereal Library, Sermons on Several Occasions, Sermon 128 "Free Grace."

52. Clarke, *Susanna Wesley*, 47.

53. Ibid., 191–192.

54. Dallimore, *Susanna Wesley*, 162.

55. Ibid., 165.

56. Clarke, *Susanna Wesley*, 208.

CHAPTER THREE: HANNAH MORE

1. Sharp, in addition to being a biblical scholar and legal beagle of the first order, came from a renowned musical family that played their music while on barges floating in the Thames. He could reportedly play two flutes at once and sometimes signed documents "G#."

2. Isaac Milner is known mainly for leading Wilberforce to faith in their chaise journey through the snowy Alps, but he was also a polymath who was the Lucasian professor at Cambridge, a lifelong academic chair held by Isaac Newton and Stephen Hawking. Milner was also physically gigantic and was a storytelling raconteur in the mold of the great Dr. Johnson.

3. Hannah More, *The Complete Works* (New York: Derby and Jackson, 1857), 1:355.

4. William Roberts, *Memoirs of the Life and Correspondence of Mrs. Hannah More* (New York: Harper and Brothers, 1834), 1:138.

5. Roberts, *Memoirs*, 1:45.

6. William Forbes, *An Account of the Life and Writings of James Beatie* (New York: Brisban and Brannan, 1807), 377.

7. Roberts, *Memoirs*, 1:146.

8. Caddell would also in 1797 publish Wilberforce's book, *A Practical View of the Prevailing Religious System of Professed Christians in the Higher and Middle Classes of This Country Contrasted With Real Christianity.*

9. Roberts, *Memoirs*, 1:77.

10. More, *Complete Works*, 1:545.

11. Samuel Johnson, *The Lives of the Most Eminent English Poets* (London: T. Longman et al, 1794), 2:247.

12. Karen Swallow Prior, *Fierce Convictions* (Nashville: Thomas Nelson, 2014), 86.

13. Ibid., 107.

14. Roberts, *Memoirs*, 1:138.

15. Ibid., 1:111.

16. Ibid., 1:291.

17. Henry Thompson, *The Life of Hannah More* (Philadelphia: E.L. Carey and A. Hart, 1838), 1:86.

18. Roberts, *Memoirs*, 1:50.

19. Prior, *Fierce Convictions*, 98.

20. John Ker Spittal, *Contemporary Criticisms of Dr. Samuel Johnson, His Works, and His Biographers* (London: John Murray, 1923), 207.

21. Prior, *Fierce Convictions*, 115.

22. Roberts, *Memoirs*, 1:281.

23. Ibid., 1:266.

24. John Pollock, *Wilberforce* (London: Constable, 1977), 64.

25. Roberts, *Memoirs*, 1:421.

26. More, *Complete Works*, 1:58.

27. Prior, *Fierce Convictions*, 141.

28. Thompson, *Life*, 1:116.

29. Roberts, *Memoirs*, 1:339.

30. Ibid., 1:339.

31. Ibid., 1:477.

32. More, *Complete Works*, 1:275.

33. Roberts, *Memoirs*, 1:455.

34. Ibid., 1:472.

35. Ibid., 1:474.

36. Ibid., 1:427.

37. Ibid., 1:346.

38. Percy Bysshe Shelley, *Essays, Letters from Abroad, Translations and Fragments* (Philadelphia: Lea and Blanchard, 1840), 1:62.

CHAPTER FOUR: SAINT MARIA OF PARIS

1. Sergei Hackel, *Pearl of Great Price* (Crestwood, NY: St. Vladimir's Seminary Press, 1965), 76.

2. Ibid., 78–79.

3. The chapel housing this icon was struck by lightning in 1888. The poor box fell to the floor and broke open, scattering its coins. Everything burned. Only the icon survived untouched, but for twelve half-kopek coins fused to its surface.

4. T. Stratton Smith, *The Rebel Nun* (Springfield, IL: Templegate, 1965), 61.

5. Hackel, *Pearl of Great Price*, 95.

6. Maria Skobstova, *Mother Maria Skobtsova: Essential Writings*, trans. Richard Pevear and Larissa Volokhonsky (Maryknoll, NY: Orbis Books, 2003), 16.

7. Ibid., 54.

8. Smith, *The Rebel Nun*, 74.

9. Ibid., 109.

10. Hackel, *Pearl of Great Price*, 5.

11. Ibid., 6.

12. Ibid., 11.

13. Skobstova, *Mother Maria Skobtsova*, 57.

14. Hackel, *Pearl of Great Price*, 15.

15. Ibid., 15.

16. Ibid., 16.

17. Smith, *The Rebel Nun*, 115.

18. Hackel, *Pearl of Great Price*, 23.

19. Skobtsova, *Mother Maria Skobtsova*, 93.

20. Ibid., 95.

21. "Metropolitan Anthony's [Sourozh Diocese, London] Memories of Mother Maria," Orthodox Christian Laity, August 19, 2002, http://archive.ocl.org/?id=12426.

22. Smith, *The Rebel Nun*, 135.

23. Hélène Arjakovsky-Klepinine, *Dimitri's Cross* (Ben Lomond, Conciliar Press, 2008), 102.

24. Skobtsova, *Mother Maria Skobtsova*, 78.

25. Ibid., 31.

26. Ibid., 109, 113, 114–115.

27. Ibid., 60.

28. Smith, *The Rebel Nun*, 122.

29. Ibid., 129.

30. Hackel, *Pearl of Great Price*, 52.

31. Grigori Benevitch, "The Saving of the Jews: The Case of Mother Maria (Scobtsova)," *Occasional Papers on Religion in Eastern Europe*, 2000, 20:1:1, http://digitalcommons.georgefox.edu/ree/vol20/iss1/1.

32. Hackel, *Pearl of Great Price*, 113.

33. Ibid., 115.

34. This group, calling themselves "German Christians," were committed Nazis who tried to reconcile National Socialist and anti-Semitic ideology with what they called "Positive Christianity." Bonhoeffer and his colleagues in the Confessing Church were their chief enemies.

35. Hackel, *Pearl of Great Price*, 108.

36. Smith, *The Rebel Nun*, 171.

37. Ibid., 209.

38. Ibid., 218.

39. Arjakovsky-Klepinine, *Dimitri's Cross*, 128.

40. Hackel, *Pearl of Great Price*, 122.

41. Ibid., 137.

42. Ibid., 130–131.

43. While the original was lost, survivors recalled its details and a reproduction was later made.

44. Hackel, *Pearl of Great Price*, 148.

45. Michael Plekon, *Living Icons* (South Bend, IN: University of Notre Dame Press, 2002), 80.

46. "The Righteous Among The Nations," http://db.yadvashem.org/righteous/family.html?language=en&itemId=4044235.

CHAPTER FIVE: CORRIE TEN BOOM

1. Corrie ten Boom, with C.C. Carlson, *In My Father's House: The Years Before the Hiding Place* (Old Tappan, NJ: Revell Company, 1976), 11–12.
2. Ibid., 16.
3. Corrie ten Boom, with Elizabeth and John Sherrill, *The Hiding Place*. (Washington Depot, CT: Chosen Books, 1971), 15.
4. Ten Boom, *In My Father's House*, 47.
5. Ibid., 133, 137.
6. Ibid., 145–146.
7. Ten Boom, *Hiding Place*, 49.
8. Ibid., 58.
9. Ibid., 61.
10. Michal Ann Goll, *Women on the Frontlines* (Shippensburg, PA: Destiny Image, 1999), 119.
11. Ten Boom, *Hiding Place*, 76–77.
12. Ibid., 83.
13. Ibid., 96.
14. Ibid.
15. Ibid., 105.
16. Ibid., 114.
17. Ibid., 115.
18. Ibid., 132.
19. Ibid., 133.
20. Ibid.
21. Ibid.
22. Ibid., 145.
23. Ibid., 146.
24. Ibid., 148.
25. Ibid., 150.
26. Ibid., 153.
27. Ibid., 154.
28. Ibid., 234.
29. Ibid., 159.
30. Corrie ten Boom, with Jamie Buckingham, *Tramp for the Lord*. (London: Hodder & Stoughton, 1975), 217–218.

31. Lawrence Baron, "Supersessionism without Contempt: The Holocaust Evangelism of Corrie ten Boom," in *Christian Responses to the Holocaust: Moral and Ethical Issues*, ed. Donald J. Dietrich (Syracuse, NY: Syracuse University Press, 2003), 127.

CHAPTER SIX: ROSA PARKS

1. Rosa Parks, *Quiet Strength: The Faith, the Hope, and the Heart of a Woman Who Changed a Nation* (Grand Rapids, MI: Zondervan, 1994), 54.

2. Douglas Brinkley, *Rosa Parks: A Life* (New York: A Penguin Life, 2000), 15.

3. Ibid., 24.

4. Ibid., 25.

5. Ibid., 35.

6. Ibid., 38.

7. Ibid., 32.

8. "Rosa Parks and the Montgomery Bus Boycott," www.africanafrican. com/folder11/world%20history1/black%20history/Rosa%20Parks.pdf.

9. 145 Cong. Rec. S3837 (daily ed. April 19, 1999) (statement of Sen. Abraham), www.gpo.gov/fdsys/pkg/CREC-1999–04–19/html/CREC-1999–04–19-pt1-PgS3837.htm.

10. Rosa Parks, *My Story* (New York: Dial Books, 1992), 100.

11. Ibid., 112.

12. Jennifer Rosenberg, "Rosa Parks Refuses to Give Up Her Bus Seat," *About.com 20th Century History*, http://history1900s.about.com/od/1950s/qt/RosaParks.htm.

13. Brinkley, *Rosa Parks*, 109.

14. Ibid.

15. Ibid., 107.

16. Ibid., 108.

17. Ibid., 109.

18. Ibid., 110.

19. Parks, *My Story*, 118.

20. Brinkley, *Rosa Parks*, 110.

21. Bettye Collier-Thomas and V. P. Franklin, *Sisters in the Struggle, African-American Women in the Civil Rights–Black Power Movement* (New York: New York University Press, 2001), 63.

22. "Overview," *The Montgomery Bus Boycott: They Changed the World*, www.montgomeryboycott.com/overview/.

23. Parks, *My Story*, 133.

24. Collier-Thomas and Franklin, *Sisters in the Struggle*, 68.

25. Juan Williams, *Eyes on the Prize: America's Civil Rights Years, 1954–1965* (New York: Viking, 1987), 76.

26. Parks, *My Story*, 140.

27. Ibid., 148.

28. Ibid., 166–167.

29. Ibid., 167.

30. Ibid., 168.

31. Ibid., 173.

32. Parks, *Quiet Strength*, 75.

33. Ibid., 16.

34. Ibid., 17.

35. Ibid., 58–59.

36. Ibid., 23.

37. Jeanne Theoharis, *The Rebellious Life of Mrs. Rosa Parks* (Boston: Beacon Press, 2013), vii.

38. Ibid.

CHAPTER SEVEN: MOTHER TERESA

1. My book about Wilberforce has been translated into Albanian, spoken by most people in the Republic of Macedonia.

2. My account of this experience can be found in *No Pressure, Mr. President: The Power of True Belief in a Time of Crisis* (Nashville: Thomas Nelson, 2012).

3. "Mother Teresa at National Prayer Breakfast," www.youtube.com/watch?v=OXn-wf5ylgo.

4. Leo-M. Maasburg, *Mother Teresa of Calcutta: A Personal Portrait* (San Francisco: Ignatius Press, 2011).

5. Kathryn Spink, *Mother Teresa: A Complete Authorized Biography* (New York: HarperOne, 2011), 8.

6. Amy Ruth, *Mother Teresa* (Minneapolis, MN: Learner Publications, 1999), 35.

7. Robert E. Barron, *The Priority of Christ: Toward a Post-Liberal Catholicism* (Grand Rapids: Brazos Press, 2007), 332.

8. Christie R. Ritter, *Mother Teresa: Humanitarian and Advocate for the Poor* (Edina, MI: ABDO, 2011), 32.

9. Spink, *Mother Teresa*, 22.

10. James Martin, *My Life with the Saints* (Chicago: Loyola Press, 2006), 166.

11. Spink, *Mother Teresa*, 35.

12. Ibid., 36.

13. Ibid., 38.

14. Maasburg, *Mother Teresa of Calcutta*, 158.

15. David Aikman, *Great Souls: Six Who Changed the Century* (Nashville: Word, 1998), 221.

16. Spink, *Mother Teresa*, 49.

17. Ibid., 86.

18. Malcolm Muggeridge, *Something Beautiful for God: Mother Teresa of Calcutta* (New York: Harper & Row, 1971), 30–31.

19. Ibid., 41–44.

20. Ibid., 17.

21. Ibid., 28.

22. Spink, *Mother Teresa*, 87.

23. Ibid., 125.

24. Ibid., 179.

25. "Mother Teresa—Nobel Lecture," *Nobelprize.org.* Nobel Media AB 201, www.nobelprize.org/nobel_prizes/peace/laureates/1979/teresa-lecture.html.

26. www.motherteresa.org/Centenary/English/Holinessisnot_MT.html.

27. Spink, *Mother Teresa*, 148.

28. Ibid., 225.

29. "Doubts, Exorcism Shine Spotlight on Mother Teresa," CNN.com/World, Sept. 7, 2001, http://edition.cnn.com/2001/WORLD/asiapcf/south/09/07/mother.teresa/.

30. Ibid., 300.

31. Joseph Langford, *Mother Teresa's Secret Fire: The Encounter that Changed Her Life and How It Can Transform Your Own* (Huntington, IN: Our Sunday Visitor Publishing Division, 2008), 31.

32. Ibid., epigraph.

Index

About the Author

Eric Metaxas is the *New York Times* #1 bestselling author of *Miracles, Bonhoeffer, Seven Men, Amazing Grace,* and more than thirty other books. He is the host of the *Eric Metaxas Show,* a nationally syndicated radio program heard in more than 120 cities around the country. ABC News has called Eric "a photogenic, witty ambassador for faith." He was the keynote speaker at the 2012 National Prayer Breakfast in Washington, DC, and he speaks to tens of thousands around the United States and internationally each year. Eric is a senior fellow and lecturer-at-large at the King's College in New York City, where he lives with his wife and daughter.

www.ericmetaxas.com